PENGUIN ⓟ CLASSICS

THE ORIGIN MYTH OF ACOMA PUEBLO

EDWARD PROCTOR HUNT was born at Acoma Pueblo in western New Mexico in mid-February 1861. Four days after his birth, he received his Indian name, "Day Break," and was raised within a traditional family. Initiated into his tribe's Katsina Society and trained toward becoming a medicine man, he was then sent to Albuquerque Indian School, where he stayed for three years. He took his Anglo name from a name inside a donated Bible. When he returned to Acoma, the elders preferred that he attend a Catholic school, at St. Catherine's in Santa Fe. After his father suddenly died, he was called back to Acoma and trained as a sacred clown, at which time he learned many of the stories that he combined into this version of the tribe's creation narrative. Over his nontraditional career, he became a storekeeper, a Wild West Show Indian with the stage name of "Big Snake," an international traveler, an anthropological consultant, and a storyteller. He died in Albuquerque in 1948.

PETER NABOKOV is a professor of American Indian Studies and World Arts and Cultures at UCLA. He is the author of *How the World Moves: The Odyssey of an American Indian Family*, *Where the Lightning Strikes: The Lives of American Indian Sacred Places*, *Restoring a Presence: American Indians and Yellowstone National Park*, *Indian Running*, *A Forest of Time: American Indian Ways of History*, *Native American Architecture* (with Robert Easton), *Architecture of Acoma Pueblo*, and *Two Leggings: The Making of a Crow Warrior*, and he edited the volume *Native American Testimony: A Chronicle of Indian-White Relations from Prophecy to the Present, 1492–2000*. He lives in Los Angeles.

EDWARD PROCTOR HUNT

The Origin Myth of Acoma Pueblo

Translated by
HENRY WAYNE WOLF ROBE HUNT *and*
WILBERT EDWARD BLUE SKY EAGLE HUNT

Edited by
MATTHEW W. STIRLING, ELSIE CLEWS PARSONS,
LESLIE A. WHITE, *and* PETER NABOKOV

Introduction by
PETER NABOKOV

PENGUIN BOOKS

PENGUIN BOOKS

An imprint of Penguin Random House LLC
375 Hudson Street
New York, New York 10014
penguin.com

First published in the United States of America under the title *Origin Myth of Acoma and
Other Records* by the Smithsonian Institution Bureau of American Ethnology 1942
This edition with an introduction and notes by Peter Nabokov published in Penguin Books 2015

Introduction and notes copyright © 2015 by Peter Nabokov

LIBRARY OF CONGRESS CATALOGING-IN-PUBLICATION DATA
Hunt, Edward Proctor, 1861–1948.
The origin myth of Acoma Pueblo / narrated by Edward Proctor Hunt ; translated by Henry
Wayne Wolf Robe Hunt and Wilbert Blue Sky Eagle Hunt ; edited by Matthew W. Stirling, Elsie
Clews Parsons, Leslie A. White, and Peter Nabokov ; introduction by Peter Nabokov.
pages cm—(Penguin classics)
Includes bibliographical references.
ISBN 978-0-14-310605-0
1. Acoma mythology.   2. Acoma Pueblo (N.M.)   I. Hunt, Wilbert Blue Sky Eagle, 1907–2007.
II. Nabokov, Peter, editor.   III. Title.
E99.A16H84 2015
978.9'91—dc23
2015004040

Set in Sabon LT Std

146028962

Contents

Preface

This version of the creation and migration story of Acoma Pueblo in western New Mexico was told in Washington, DC, to scholars at the Smithsonian Institution's Bureau of American Ethnology in the fall of 1928. Its narrator was a sixty-seven-year-old Indian man originally from Acoma Pueblo. His native name was Gaire, meaning "Day Break," but the name he acquired at Albuquerque Indian School was Edward Proctor Hunt. Translating for him was a son, Henry Wayne "Wolf Robe" Hunt, while a younger son, Wilbert Edward "Blue Sky Eagle" Hunt, assisted with translating the songs that were integral to the myth. In addition, there were Mr. Hunt's wife, Marie "Morning Star" Valle Hunt, and Philip "Silver-tongue" Sanchez, originally from Santa Ana Pueblo. Transcribing the myth were archaeologist and recently appointed "chief" of the Bureau of American Ethnology Dr. Matthew W. Stirling and a young visiting British anthropologist, Dr. C. Daryll Forde.

After fourteen years of additional editing by some of the American Southwest's most respected researchers—Leslie A. White, Elsie Clews Parsons, and Franz Boas—the narrative was published in 1942 by the U.S. Government Printing Office as Bulletin 135 of the Bureau of American Ethnology, *Origin Myth of Acoma and Other Records*. In its preface, the narrator and assistants were not named; Stirling was the author of record.

Over the years, this relatively obscure publication became one of the most cited sources on Pueblo Indian worldview and narrative tradition. Students of mythology, Pueblo culture, and the region quoted from it, wove it into their theories, and incorporated it into anthologies, interpretations of Pueblo history and society, and university courses on myth and oral tradition. A newly edited version that reinserted material that had been excised, offered a biographical profile of its narrator and his assistants, and rendered the text more accessible, seemed overdue.

First and foremost, I am grateful to the late Wilbert Hunt for background on his father, for memories of his family's travels and their time in Washington, and for his blessing to prepare this edition of his father's version. Second, I am indebted to the late James Glenn, archivist at the Smithsonian's National Anthropological Archives, who showed me the Frances Densmore and Wolf Robe Hunt files that confirmed Edward Hunt as the narrator and began my research into his family. Mary Powell and Marta Weigle of Ancient City Press had published my work on Acoma's architecture, derived from the 1934 Historic American Buildings Survey Project, and encouraged this republication. For time and resources to research the myth's background, edit its text, and investigate the family's background, I thank Princeton University for a fall 2006 Stewart Fellowship, Pasadena's Huntington Library for a 2007–08 residency Mellon Fellowship, the John Simon Guggenheim Foundation for a 2008–09 fellowship, UCLA's Faculty Grants Program, and New Mexico's State Records Center and Archives grant program.

I am also indebted to the American Philosophical Society, the Smithsonian Institution's National Anthropological Archives, Ann Arbor's University of Michigan Special Collections Library, Pasadena's Southwest Museum, and the University of New Mexico's Center for Southwest Research and Special Collections for access to materials directly related to the history behind this publication and the careers of the Hunt family.

Individuals who have been essential to my work on this publication are Susan Bergholz, Alfred Bush, Don Cosentino, Linda Feldman, Karen Finney, Jim Glenn, Louis Hieb, Eddie Hunt, Steve Karr, Paul Kroskrity, Robert Leopold, Jay Miller, Alfonso Ortiz, Mo Palmer, Bill Peace, Patrick Polk, Roy Ritchie, Gregory Schachner, Bill Truettner, Ken Wade, and Kim Walters.

Introduction

THE CREATION OF CREATION MYTHS

Stories about the origins of any community's universe—its gods, spirits, heroes, and landscapes; its beginnings, wanderings, sufferings, and fulfillments—are the most important accounts any society can tell itself about itself. They are its divine charter, declaration of independence, constitution, and bill of rights all wrapped into one guiding narrative. Like a cosmic compass, they set its course. They provide models for its institutions and remind its people who they are, why they exist, and how they fit into their grand scheme of things. As foundational narratives, these stories are sometimes dramatized, usually for members only and at regular moments on the community's ceremonial calendar. They are also recalled as scripts or formulas for conducting proper rituals. And they can be revisited whenever their teachings seem most relevant.

Constituting what some call "original instructions," such myths inform their constituencies how to behave and move forward in order to remain their unique social selves. They are declarations of all that the culture considers primary, true, and essential. Contrary to the popular use of the term as human invention or falsehood, "myths" of this magnitude are usually considered as sacredly revealed, repositories of ultimate truths, and arbiters of existential questions.

Most of the world's major narratives of cultural genesis have cohered over time out of a cluster of separate and often older narratives. And commonly, those separate stories, focusing on the establishment of this or that constituent group or cultural practice, wind up being told in multiple ways. Sometimes this is because, through the invocation of these myths, individuals, societal divisions, or priestly elites are

making some case or claim and hence they might add, sub-
tract, or alter elements in them.

For these reasons it is usually futile to search for a single
originating or seminal version of any culture's creation story.
They have grown out of portions told by different people
at different times for different reasons. Whenever outsiders
study any culture's origin myth, they generally try to com-
pare the fullest array of what are called a myth's *variant* expressions, whether in lengthy or fragmentary forms, in order
to identify their most abiding and widespread elements and
to understand the various influences that may have weighed
on them over time.

Throughout human history, it has been out of such bun-
dles of separate stories that gifted narrators or big-thinking
synthesizers, special-interest groups, or nationalizing com-
mittees have tried to compose single, dominating accounts of
creation, the emergence of human society, and the relation-
ships between gods and humans.

The culture keepers and storytellers behind such master
myths have hailed from various backgrounds. Some were men
and women of a rare philosophical or historical bent, or they
possessed exceptional memories or storytelling gifts. Some suffered a physical impairment that kept them home, so their full-
time job became as community historian, memory bank, or
renowned bard. Others may have occupied a privileged religious status or played a noteworthy intellectual or political
role in their community. And then there are those individuals
whose cultural exposure was so broad that they enjoyed access
to an unusually wide range of separate accounts. Such seems to
have been the case with Edward Hunt, the narrator of this version of the Acoma creation story.

Different motivations have driven storytellers to compile
such authoritative accounts. Given the powerful impact of creation myths on how people believe and act, and the likelihood
of multiple versions and the contradictions among them, it is
inevitable that some have maintained that theirs should be the
true or dominating one. Sometimes select groups or scribal
specialists authorized a single orthodox or "revised standard"

account and attempted to sideline or even outlaw all others. But for an outsider, all versions tell us something about the complicated and unruly strands, stories, and histories that reveal the community's development and its evolving sense of itself.

In the remote past, the activity of transmitting central stories and their teachings from one generation to another happened orally, in line with the mouth-to-ear origins of human storytelling. These transmissions introduced all manner of additions and changes. Following the oral transmissions and subsequent elaborations and additions of more stories sometimes came their consolidations into single versions. Often their contents were altered even more by their exposure to creation stories from other cultures, whether the changes were adopted by choice or imposed by conquest.

Then or thereafter, these oral narratives were further condensed as they were fixed into some form of writing or print. And following their conversions from oral to written media, origin stories frequently underwent a fourth transformation. They wove their way into distant societies through the error-prone work of translation from one language to another.

Whether these transformative processes were imposed upon the traditions of small-scale, preindustrial, face-to-face cultures or contributed to the sacred texts of complex societies that produced the so-called world religions, the evolution from oral to written forms usually took a while—often hundreds, sometimes a thousand years or more. In the case of this Pueblo Indian myth, however, its summarizing, narrating, translating, and transcription was completed in about eight weeks. Yet the stories that it contained had been accumulating in the mind of its narrator since he was a child at Acoma Pueblo in western New Mexico.

THE WORLD THIS MYTH CREATED

The society that emerged out of this creation-and-migration narrative is found in today's Valencia County in western New

Mexico, about sixty miles west of present-day Albuquerque. As established in the myth's closing scenes, the village called Ha'ako, commonly referred to today as "Old Acoma" but advertised in tourist campaigns as "Sky City," sits on the flat summit of a 375-foot-high sandstone mesa. Its earthen-colored buildings and oversize San Estevan church appear to grow out of the rock itself. The seventeen-acre mesa top is surrounded by clusters of immense sandstone monoliths. This rocky ensemble sits in the midst of a flat plain whose backdrop of low cliffs is interrupted by broad valleys. To the east rises Katzimo, or Enchanted Mesa, whose summit was once occupied by Acoma's ancestors. This panorama makes for one of the most dramatic town sites in the western hemisphere.

Encompassing a 245,672-acre reservation, with its old mesa-top village and two satellite communities, Acoma Pueblo is one of nineteen autonomous Pueblo Indian tribes in New Mexico and Arizona. Because these towns centered around open plazas and their buildings were multistory, condominium-like structures built of mud and stone, the earliest Spanish visitors in the sixteenth century found them familiar and called them *pueblos*.

At nearly seven thousand feet above sea level, with an annual rainfall of between only eleven inches and sixteen inches a year, the high arid desert that drops eastward from the Colorado Plateau is a tough place to make a living. The people of Acoma combined dry and irrigation farming techniques, developed individual and collective hunting strategies, and gathered a host of wild foods. Even then, drought, famine, enemy attacks, and European-derived diseases made for a precarious existence.

Today's pueblos are direct descendants of cultures whose ancient ruins can be visited in the cliffs of Mesa Verde and the creek bottom of Chaco Canyon. Scholars often divide these pueblos into the Western villages—embracing the Hopi, Zuni, Laguna, and Acoma territories—and the Eastern or Rio Grande Pueblos, which extend from Taos Pueblo near the Colorado state line, down to Isleta Pueblo, just south of Albuquerque.

In contrast to "plaza-centered" pueblo villages, which cluster around a communal space, Acoma is a "street-type" pueblo. Facing its three alleylike byways are eight "houseblocks," with its cross-axial plaza more a widened corridor between two streets. Although much remodeled today, with one-story, single-family houses increasingly crowding the mesa rim, the old-time two- or three-story blocks stepped back with each tier. In the practice of passive solar heating, their southern exposure allowed the sandstone-and-adobe walls to absorb the sun's warmth by day and radiate it inside during the night. Combined with small, relatively smokeless fires, their cocoonlike sleeping rooms kept families comfortable over the winter. In warmer months, their people dried meat and native fruits in the sun and visited and socialized beneath an open sky, often in the shade of dividing walls on their roof terraces.

Acoma is positioned in the center of a Pueblo Indian world that extends from the Rio Grande River in New Mexico to the Painted Desert in Arizona. Its social and religious institutions reflect the influences of both its eastern and western neighbors. It is one of the seven Indian pueblos that speak dialects of the Keresan language. Like its western neighbors, the Zuni and Hopi, the community features a clan-based society and contains multiple rectangular *kivas*, or sacred meeting rooms. But Acoma's medicine-men societies enjoy the kind of prominence usually found among the eastern, or Rio Grande, pueblos. While the pueblo's farmers practiced the "dry farming" methods of the West—coaxing irregular plots of maize out of apparently waterless, sandy basins—at their satellite "farming villages" they also maintained irrigation ditches, as were more commonly found along the Jemez and Rio Grande river valleys to the east.

Today the people of Acoma have largely relocated off the mesa, occupying housing projects and dispersed homes in and around the colony villages of Acomita and McCartys. Some have resettled in towns like Grants and Albuquerque. Over the winter, a few families are assigned to reside on the summit to maintain a symbolic presence and fulfill ritual duties. But most Acoma families still retain house and room rights on the mesa, where they return for the yearly round of ceremonies and feast days. Some festivities are open to the public, but others are off-limits to outsiders.

A living architectural shrine, Old Acoma remains the spiritual pivot of the tribe's universe.

While Acoma Pueblo may be, as its tour guides claim, the oldest continuously occupied settlement in North America, archaeologists allow more cautiously that the "Acoma cultural province" has received residents for a very long time. First were stone-and-bone tool-using Paleo-Indians who lived in the region more than ten thousand years ago. Around 5500 BC, the extended residence of Archaic period hunter-gatherers began; they later settled on mesa tops and valleys and adopted gardening as a secondary food source. By AD 400, they were evolving into the culture now referred to as Ancestral Pueblo. Their farming practices, belief system, and fertility and harvest rituals developed in the "great house" ruins of the Four Corners region. But a convergence of factors—drought high among them—cast their inhabitants on various roads toward the south and southeast. As early as AD 950, some of these early migrants appeared along the San Jose and Puerco river valleys, with Acoma mesa itself settled by the 1400s.

The village's written history began in 1540, when a scribe on Hernando de Alvarado's expedition into the Southwest wrote home about this "strange place built upon solid rock." He described its defensible location, and at least seven ladder-and-stone-step trails to the summit where piles of rocks were readied to rain down on invaders like him. Near the edge of the mesa, freshwater cisterns held ample snowmelt and rainwater. Stored within the houseblocks lay enough dried corn, meat, and fruit to sustain its people for up to four years.

Over the following decades, the Spanish traded for Acoma food and sought to convert the Indians to Christianity. Relations soured in 1598 after Mexican-born Don Juan de Oñate, authorized to obtain the pueblo's submission to the Spanish crown, developed doubts about its loyalty. His suspicions were confirmed when his nephew Juan de Zaldívar and most of his platoon were killed by Acoma arrows, clubs, and rocks. In retaliation, Oñate dispatched Juan's brother, Vicente, with seventy armor-clad soldiers and their cannons.

In late January 1599, the Spanish committed one of the bloodiest revenges in southwestern history. The three-day punishment of Acoma ended with more than six hundred dead Indians and a village in rubble. Documents describe the Spanish sentencing survivors over twenty-five years of age to amputation of a foot, with other males and females between twelve and twenty-five condemned to twenty years of servitude. By then its population was down to around fifteen hundred members. Despite these brutalities, thirty years later a priest named Fray Juan Ramírez somehow rallied townsfolk (tribal tradition says forcibly conscripted them) to reconstruct the church's ten-foot-thick adobe walls, harvest its ponderosa pine rafters from the San Mateo Mountains, and complete the forty-foot-high roof for New Mexico's largest church, San Estevan del Rey, whose much rebuilt and restored edifice still towers over the mesa.

Over the next half century, life at a weakened Acoma remained relatively isolated and peaceful. Within other Indian pueblos that lay closer to Spanish scrutiny, a wave of religious suppression against "heathen" practices intensified. Sacred kivas were invaded, ceremonies disrupted, spirit masks and ritual regalia burned, and native priests and medicine men publicly whipped. Among them was a religious leader from San Juan Pueblo named Po'pay. With rebels from other villages, he secretly organized what became the All-Pueblo Revolt. One day in early August 1680, most of the loosely connected Pueblo Indian world, spreading across four hundred miles, rose up against Catholic missions and Spanish ranchos. In this most successful of American Indian uprisings, Acoma hurled its priest, Lucas Maldonado, to death on the rocks below. All told, nineteen Catholic missionaries and nearly four hundred Spanish colonists were killed; the survivors fled into old Mexico.

Although the region was reconquered by the Spanish twelve years later, the authority of Catholicism was never the same.

The Pueblo kivas and Christian churches came to conduct parallel, sometimes entwined, celebrations, but native ways of belief, ritual, and theocratic organization now held sway. By 1820, as Mexico took over the American Southwest, and thirty years later, when the United States assumed control, Acoma's population kept dropping. Yet its people maintained their time-honored rhythms of growing corn, squash, and tobacco; hunting for rabbits and antelope; harvesting wild foods; and fulfilling the ceremonial cycle that regulated their lives.

The next threat to Acoma's isolation was the Santa Fe Railway, which cut across Acoma and Laguna pueblo lands in the early 1880s. Pueblo women began selling pottery along the tracks, and Indian dances and arts were advertised by railroad publicists. Generations of tourists became exposed to what one writer has called "the romantic inflation" of Pueblo life.

In the early 1920s, Acoma joined with fellow Pueblos in successfully opposing federal legislation that attempted to legalize the thousands of non-Indian squatters. Over the next forty years, its population steadily increased. Since the 1970s, the pueblo has attracted thousands to the tribe's casino-and-hotel complex at Acomita off Interstate 40.

But Acoma remains ambivalent about embracing a modernizing world. At the foot of the mesa, visitors see exhibits and orientation films at a two-million-dollar museum before a tram takes them up to the old village for a tour with native guides. Outsiders are welcome to attend the September 2 annual Acoma Fiesta, but for key rituals and dances in their old religious calendar, the old village is closed off. Always hovering over the community is the challenge of how to remain a semisovereign, religiously private, Keresan-speaking traditional Pueblo people within a wired, multiethnic, open-access world.

EDWARD PROCTOR HUNT:
THE STORY OF THE NARRATOR

To appreciate this version of Acoma's origin myth, one must review its narrator's unconventional career. Born four months before the onset of the Civil War and dying three years after the end of World War II, his successive names were Day Break, Edward Proctor Hunt, and Chief Big Snake. While the 1942 publication of the myth attributed the work only to "a group of Pueblo Indians from Acoma and Santa Ana visiting Washington [in the fall of 1928]," a glance at a 1957 Smithsonian report on Pueblo Indian music suggests the storyteller's identity. Its frontispiece featured a photograph of the Edward Hunt family troupe in their "show Indian" outfits of Plains Indian war bonnets and heavily beaded shirts, vests, and leggings.

The stories that Edward Hunt braided into this narrative were so packed with detail because he was so steeped in his tribe's lore. He was the stepson of a Fire Society medicine man but regarded the man as his father for the rest of his life. Four days after birth he received the first of his four initiatory experiences. His body was held up, or "given," to the rising sun, and he was named Gaire, meaning "First Light of Dawn," or Day Break.

Next, like most Pueblo boys, around the age of five or six he was inducted into the Katsina Society. That training taught him the mythic origins of the rain-bringing supernaturals called Katsinas. They were spirits of the ancestors who lived in the clouds and mediated between human and cosmic worlds. They brought rain, health, and all good things, and were impersonated by initiated members only. Behind their masks and regalia, the boy learned, were his own relatives and neighbors. The injunction to keep this secret was driven home by whippings with yucca staves. Katsina rituals also taught Day Break songs and prayers and life lessons that were reinforced by seasonal ceremonies and stories told over long winter nights.

His third ritual experience was less predictable. When Day Break was around ten, a bucking horse knocked him unconscious; he seemed dead to the world. The family prepared

him for burial in the *campo santo*, the old low-walled ceme-
tery that lies in front of San Estevan. When rays of sunlight
woke him up, the lad's near-death experience signaled his
candidacy for a medicine men's society, with its tough training and ritual duties.

Day Break's life might have unfolded in this traditional
vein but for the arrival in late 1880 of a Presbyterian missionary who persuaded a number of parents, his included,
to release their children to a new Indian boarding school in
Albuquerque. There the boy's hair was cut, his body clad in
a Civil War–style uniform, and he began a regimen of dor-
mitory life, marching drills, and language and math classes.
He helped to construct the school's new building, maintained its vegetable garden, sang in the choir, prayed before
meals, attended Sunday services, and was forbidden to speak
his language. One day the school received a box of donated
clothes. In the pocket of a coat received by Day Break was a
Bible with a note that allowed the finder to take its owner's
name: Edward Proctor Hunt.

But three years later, Catholic authorities, jealous of Presbyterian claims to their flock, pressured his parents to with-
draw him. Edward rode a flatcar home on the new Santa Fe
railway. With other boarding school returnees, he was taken
into a kiva and horsewhipped for speaking English, having
short hair, wearing leather shoes, and following white ways.

Then Edward found himself bound for a second institution, St. Catherine's Indian Industrial School in Santa Fe,
which had just been founded by Catholic missionary (later
to become America's second saint) and Philadelphia heiress
Katharine Drexel. Here Edward used skills learned at Albuquerque to help build its original classrooms and dorms as
well. But his stay lasted less than a year. His stepfather's
death in August 1887 returned the young man home to
Acoma and a final initiation. As eldest son and pursuant to
the old man's dying wish, Edward was indoctrinated into the
Koshares, Acoma's brotherhood of sacred clowns. It was during this lengthy training that he learned a major portion of
the origin myth he retells in these pages.

When Edward fell in love with Marie Valle, a daughter of one of Acoma's most prominent families, her father took objection. This may have been because both she and Edward belonged to Acoma's Sun clan, which made them almost siblings. Or perhaps it was because she was pregnant, although normally that was not a problem where large families absorbed most newborns. Or possibly it was because their families were so socially distant; his stepfather was a poor medicine man often dependent on the charity of clients. Nor was Edward's standing helped by his growing reluctance, as a closeted convert to Christianity, to participate in the more esoteric aspects of the pueblo's ritual life.

After a shotgun ceremony at nearby San Rafael, Marie's father dropped off the newlyweds near the eastern edge of the Malpais, a forbidding 114,000-acre volcanic wilderness that sprawls between the Acoma and Zuni Pueblo territories. They set up camp in a crudely roofed rock shelter, and for three years here they raised the first three sons of their eventual twelve children.

But banishment from one tribe was followed by his rescue by another. In 1885, Marie Hunt's older sister, Juana, married into a mercantile family of five German Jewish brothers. Hailing from Prussia, the Bibos had immigrated one by one to western New Mexico. This union gained Solomon Bibo, Juana's husband, access to her influential Acoma family and the village's leading Antelope clan. It also brought Edward Hunt an unusual brother-in-law. Fluent in Acoma, Zuni, Navajo, Spanish, German, Yiddish, and English, "Don Solomon" Bibo became an effective trader and networker with the outside world.

Exploiting his connections with the Valle family, Solomon's fortunes rose. Before long, through shady maneuverings, he even became the tribe's largest landowner. For three terms he even served as its governor, hence his popular characterization as the first "Jewish Indian chief." Although Solomon's involvement in Acoma political life was not without controversy, his loyalty to his new family brought young Edward under his wing. At the Bibo trading post in the nearby

Hispanic village of Cubero, Edward swept floors; inventoried goods; learned to restock at supply warehouses in Albuquerque; became conversant in English, Spanish, Navajo, and a bit of German; and was inspired to become a shopkeeper and entrepreneur on his own.

When Solomon and Juana left New Mexico for San Francisco around 1898, Edward Hunt stepped into the commercial vacuum. At his Acomita general store, he provided information for a stream of writers, anthropologists, and photographers. Edward S. Curtis, Charles F. Lummis, Elsie Clews Parsons, Leslie A. White, and others owed much of their information and images to him. Wrote famous photographer Edward S. Curtis in 1923, when acknowledging Hunt's help, "Excepting Zuni and Hopi, he is the only Pueblo informant with whom it was not necessary to work in seclusion and under a pledge of secrecy."

Hunt's role as an outspoken culture broker and successful businessman, his reputation as a "progressive" Indian, and his unwillingness to let his boys join Acoma's kiva groups clashed with the tribe's conservative elders. Tensions peaked in 1918; the Hunts agreed to move away. As if unwilling to make a clean break with native life, however, they were formally adopted into Santa Ana Pueblo, a Keresan-speaking pueblo closer to the Rio Grande River. But Edward's independent spirit and Christian leanings caused friction there as well. In 1924, the Hunt family packed up and moved into an Albuquerque suburb.

By now his enterprising son Henry "Wolf Robe" Hunt had contacted the Oklahoma-based Miller Brothers 101 Ranch Circus. The last of the great Wild West Shows to tour Europe, the Millers were subcontracted by the Sarrasani Circus, based in Dresden, Germany, to supply Indians for their 1926–28 "Festival of All Nations" tour. Dressing up as a Plains tribesman and redubbed "Chief Big Snake" by the Millers, Edward along with his sons Wilbert and Henry, performed war dances and chased stagecoaches around arenas in Germany, Belgium, France, and Italy.

This time abroad may have freed Edward to gather his

memories and compile Acoma's creation story as his independent mind saw fit. Perhaps telling this narrative was also
a way for the Hunts to *recenter* themselves once they returned home. Whatever their motivations, six months or so
after returning to America the family showed up in Washington, DC. In late August 1928, Edward began narrating
the myth, first to visiting British anthropologist C. Daryll
Forde, then with the brand-new "chief" of the Smithsonian
Institution's Bureau of American Ethnology, Matthew W.
Stirling.

For this task he was uniquely qualified. As a medicine
man's son, an initiate into the Katsina Society, a candidate for
becoming a healer himself, a member of the hunter's society
(for killing a bear), and an initiated sacred clown, Edward's
exposure to Acoma's esoteric lore was broader than most.

In Washington, Edward shared what he knew of his people's
world, the tribe's ancestral locations, the creation of its charac-
teristic animals and plants, and other features of western New
Mexico's cultural ecology. His exposure to Catholic and Protestant texts added echoes from Christian cosmology—people
made "in the image" of God, creation by "the word," tempta-
tion by an evil serpent, committing "a sin," and a universal
flood. Not trained to identify or analyze all that they were
hearing, Forde and Stirling found themselves also recording a
medley of Acoma genres—sacred creation stories; magical
songs, prayers, and side plots; and stories of primordial migrations, legendary wanderings, and the tribe's ultimate arrival at
its current location as a distinctive ethnic group.

For about two months, the Hunts appear to have worked
almost every day. Both of Edward's sons—twenty-six-year-
old Henry Wayne "Wolf Robe" Hunt and twenty-one-year-
old Wilbert "Blue Sky Eagle" Hunt—aided in translating the
basic text as well as the songs that were an integral part of it.
The fourth member of their group, Philip Sanchez, adopted
from the Pueblo of Santa Ana and nicknamed "Silvertongue"
for his beautiful voice, was coached so the Smithsonian could
record them. In addition, Henry, an aspiring artist, drew pictures to illustrate the document.

After the Washington sojourn, the Hunt family made Albuquerque its home base but traveled widely. Over the Depression years, they exploited the country's passion for Indian lore, patching together a living as entertainers and educators for Boy Scout groups and school districts throughout the South and Midwest. By the 1940s, Edward and Marie had retired to their suburban Albuquerque home while their children created their own careers, which included work as telephone linemen, railway shopmen, jewelry makers, touring showmen, and trading post proprietors along Route 66 between Oklahoma, New Mexico, and even California.

Five years before his father's death from stomach cancer on February 13, 1948, Wolf Robe Hunt learned from his Tulsa, Oklahoma, newspaper that the Smithsonian had recently published Edward Hunt's version of the Acoma origin myth. He wrote his scholar friend, the linguist John P. Harrington, for copies for himself, his dad, and "my younger brother Blue Sky Eagle Wilbert, who is with the army somewhere." Some years later, not knowing that the old man had died, he wrote Wolf Robe again. Unaware that photographer Edward S. Curtis and ethnomusicologist Frances Densmore had publicly named his father as one of their key informants, in his response Wolf Robe expressed concern that Harrington protect his family's identity by not talking about their Smithsonian work. "As for myself," Henry said, "I am away from home, and have been for a number of years, although I visit each year. I feel as I were merely an interpreter for my Dad." Then he added, as if privy to the personal toll on Edward Proctor Hunt of passing through such a gauntlet of identities, "Of course we know no one can hurt Dad now."

THE STORIES EDWARD TOLD

Edward's account of the ethnogenesis of the Acoma people forefronted them as the earth's original humans, their ecology as the earth's first landscape, and their mesa-top village as "the center of the world." His narrative followed two sisters, "Mothers," as they climbed upward through three underworlds until emerging upon this earthly plain. It traced the creative work of one of them, Iatiku, as she guided her Indian children to create their world and culture and launch their migratory search for a permanent home.

Of the eight traditional myth types for world creation, which folklorist Anna Birgitta Rooth identified across North America, Edward's narrative exemplifies the drama of the Emergence, which predominates across the Southwest. Most Pueblo peoples suggest that their first appearance on the new earth's surface occurred at the mythic site of Shipapu, located in the so-called Four Corners area, where the states of New Mexico, Arizona, Colorado, and Utah intersect.

Part 1, "Iatiku's World," opens in darkness, three levels below the earth. Up above the earth, the sun and other features of our world already exist. Almost as an aside, we learn the world was born when a supreme progenitor hurled a blood clot into space. Less interested in ultimate or metaphysical beginnings, however, the narrative quickly turns to cultural unfoldings.

From below the place called Shipapu, two supernatural sisters climb a series of trees toward the light. Guiding them is a female spirit, Tsichtinako, or "Thought Woman." After teaching them their language, she hands baskets to them. These contain seeds to plant as well as animal effigies representing the many creatures that they will bring to life.

The girls present a dramatic contrast. Iatiku, or "Bringing to Life," is the elder. Darker skinned and a slower thinker, she belongs to the Corn clan. Nautsiti, or "More of Everything in the Basket," is lighter complected and has a quicker mind, and she chooses the Sun clan. She is described as lazy, greedy, and rash, Iatiku as industrious, forbearing, and gentle. Nautsiti's basket contains foreign items—domesticated animals and plants, metals, written words; Iatiku's holds features of the environment for sustaining the Acoma people to come.

Now unfolds an inventory of creation, the myth's litany of the first this and the first that. As they mature, the sisters learn about the sun's movement, how night follows day, how to orient themselves in the four directions, and how to use fire, corn, and salt so as to cook and feed themselves. They plant seeds to feed the animals, make mountains to support the trees that they will cut to roof their homes, and plant other seeds to feed themselves. Through song they animate the fetishes so as to create game animals, which will feed the fetishes that they bring to life as prey animals. From birds to fish, turtles to water snakes, gradually they bring the world alive with creatures and places.

After Nautsiti is impregnated by a rainbow snake, she bears twin sons. Taking one of them, she heads east and there produces white people. Back at Shipapu, the other son grows up and marries his aunt, Iatiku. Their offspring will parent the Acoma people. Iatiku then groups the successive generations into the clans that eventually will number varyingly between a dozen and twenty.

With the spirit Tsichtinako abandoning her, Iatiku must create the rest of Acoma cosmology and culture on her own. She establishes the spirits of the four directions, who will dispense the four seasons; assigns Katsina spirits to rule the clouds; and teaches the new people how to summon them with prayer sticks. With magical words she creates their distinctive pueblo architecture—their domestic houses, central dance plaza, and ceremonial kivas. Instituting a men's hunting society, she sets rules for the killing and butchering of game and creates new fetishes and rituals to help hunters be successful.

From generating and nurturing, Iatiku moves to governing. She establishes the offices of War Chief and Country Chief. When an evil snake reappears with plague, she institutes the five medicine mens' societies with their altars. They learn to use ritual objects so as to alter the course of events, bring the near dead back to life, and even make rain during severe droughts.

To add spice to human life, Iatiku introduces a counterforce—sacred clowns, called Koshari. They behave boorishly, interrupt sacred activities, mimic dignitaries, do things back-ward, and provide relief from the seriousness of ritual life. They teach people to have fun: to hold public dances, play ball games, and run kick stick races.

Having armed her people with this foundation, Iatiku sends them to their next village location, at the place known as White House—speculated to be today's ruins of Chaco Canyon or Aztec, New Mexico. But there the diversions she taught them prove their downfall. The men become addicted to a hide-the-stick gambling game, whose songs disrespect other men's wives and even insult Iatiku herself. Hurt and an-gered, Iatiku prepares to depart, but not before alluding to the prospect of her own death; only in the afterworld will she re-unite with them. Finally, she leaves instructions so the people can find their ultimate home, Ha'ako, which lies to the south. Abandoned by both Iatiku and her Katsinas, the people suffer drought and famine until a "good man" saves them.

Element by element, each in proper sequence, this section has produced the Acoma physical world. Artifact by artifact and practice by practice, it has also created their cultural world. Covenants have been decreed between humans and spirits and between humans and nature. Now Iatiku's children possess cosmological principles, survival skills, religious and political practices, rituals for healing, a social identity, and an ethical structure. Future rituals by humans will recapitulate the symbols and acts that are this section's dramatic arc.

So her people will know when they have reached their destination, Iatiku instructs early on that when they believe they have reached Ha'ako, they must yell out loud. A clear echo is the signal that they have finally arrived. In addition, she gave them two eggs, one plain and whitish, the other a beautiful blue; from one will come crows, from the other parrots. Upon reaching Ha'ako they are to divide into two groups by choosing between the eggs; one band will stay and the other will continue traveling southward.

Bereft of Iatiku's guidance and the Katsinas' support, the peo-ple finally arrive near Ha'ako, or present-day Acoma mesa. Until now, they have escaped the consequences of their bad behavior. Will impulsive human nature disturb their lives again?

The opening of part 2, "Birth of the War Twins," has a familiar ring. Much as Nautsiti was impregnated by wet drops from the Rainbow Serpent, now the Sun god impregnates a young girl with piñon nuts. The duo of Iatiku and her absent sister, and the latter's two boys, are joined by a third pair of newborns, Masewi and Oyoyewi, sons of the Sun. When their protective energies are needed, they are exalted as the Hero Twins. But when their ferocity goes too far, they become threats to community stability.

The boys mature unusually fast and acquire remarkable skill with weapons, first as hunters, later as warriors. Eager to meet their Sun father, they are aided by Spider Woman (apparently an avatar of the spirit Tsichtinako, who originally helped the two girls). She guides them in their magical journey to the Sun's home in the sky. They must endure tests before their Sun father acknowledges his paternity, praises their mettle, and grants them superhuman killing and healing powers.

At the beginning of part 3, "The War Twins' World," harmony at White House has been restored and the War Twins are living peacefully among the people. From Iatiku's children of myth, the people have transformed into a historical band of migrants who must take responsibility for their lives.

But a disrespectful younger generation upsets things once again. They revive the gambling game with its rowdy songs and mocking imitations of Katsinas. The spirits retaliate, causing a terrible war between spirits and humans that seems to be unparalleled in the annals of pueblo mythology. Rallying to their community's side, the Twins help to kill nearly all the Katsinas. Although they come back to life, their human victims do not. Traumatized, the survivors face a dilemma. How can mortals and supernaturals possibly interact after such destruction? Their planes of existence are complementary and interdependent, yet clearly they must dwell physically apart. Then the Katsina Chief comes up with a brilliant solution.

A sacred drama will mix ritual, stagecraft, masking, and the willing suspension of disbelief. But impersonating spirits is no simple matter. Participants must become more than actors. As described in many Indian folktales, bad behavior or improper conduct of rituals runs the risk of leaving them permanently stuck between realms. During their masked visits in the plazas, streets, and kivas, the impersonated spirits bring otherworldly powers into a human community. The gravity of such appearances is counterbalanced by the levity of sacred clowns. They allow the townsfolk to enjoy vicariously the sort of fun-making that once cost them so dearly. As the clowns mock the Katsinas, everyone's smiles amount to a collective release. Yet these "delight makers," as early ethnologist Adolph Bandelier labeled them, borrowing from a phrase by the famous scholar Frank Hamilton Cushing, also distract the people from observing the Katsinas too closely, lest the true identities of the individuals who are personifying them be disclosed.

For the next misfortune to befall the people, however, a "disease with blisters," there is no retrospective explanation; no one appears to have misbehaved. Indeed, history may have intervened here, in the form of the early sixteenth-century smallpox epidemic, which native demographer Russell Thornton suggests spread from northern Mexico to the Southwest in 1520. To counter the plague, the people migrate to Sage Basin, reestablishing their buildings, the plaza, and their kivas.

Then a visit by some Katsinas revives the bad behavior of disrespectful men yet again. To avoid a repeat of the earlier bloodbath, the village War Chief comes up with another solution through the medium of performance. The community will reenact the terrible war with the Katsinas. Its stage prop will be a curtain of dried buffalo hides, representing the village walls. Some will play the part of invading Katsinas, others the defending villagers. The War Twins will participate as well. In the ensuing melee, those performing as invading Katsinas will pretend to die, but the actual mockers will pay with their lives.

After angry relatives of the dead split off, the rest move to yet another location, Tule Lake. A new medicine society purges the site, a new village emerges, but drought and famine return nonetheless. Falling back on their old role as community saviors, the Twins sneak into Katsina country to steal weather-controlling medicine. The Katsinas retaliate with storms and floods. The people save themselves by ascending a mountain. Only when the Twins shoot arrows at the waves do they subside.

From now on, nothing will deflect the wandering people from their search for their predestined home. Carrying Iatiku's oracular eggs, they bypass the site of future Laguna Pueblo, camp at Antelope Range, then visit Hardwood Pass, and finally reach Katzimo (also known as Enchanted Mesa). All the while they maintain the cycle of dancing, praying, and planting associated with the agricultural year.

For the Twins, one adventure remains. Sounding as if Hunt has inserted a folktale into his epic, the two clash with the evil gambling spirit of South Mountain. Humbled at last by this chastening experience, they are beset by the same kind of fears as ordinary human beings.

Finally arriving at Ha'ako, the people locate the clear echo and learn who is to stay and who must travel southward by choosing between the two eggs. Thinking that by picking the attractive blue egg they will be associating with the beautiful parrots, most select the blue. But when they crack it, crows burst forth. While this contingent will remain at Ha'ako, those aligned with the white egg, which yields colorful parrots, splinter off, presumably into old Mexico.

Accepting punishment for their impetuous actions, the Twins submit to a purification ritual. This institutes yet a third ceremony for the people to practice in the years ahead. The scalps of their victims are propitiated so enemy spirits cannot haunt their killers, and at the same time so Pueblo warriors can be honored for bravery. Disconsolate about facing a future as inactive commoners, the Twins disappear into a rock near the mesa's edge.

Still encamped at the mesa's foot, the people prepare for

their ascent to its summit. Rather than conducting their arrival in a spirit of triumph, they make this final move with reverential, stately care. First the medicine men clear ants, centipedes, and snakes from the surface. A main Rainbow Trail up the mesa is purified and marked by prayer sticks. Additional offerings are deposited where the seven kivas are to be constructed. After building the houseblocks, Country Chief and the Antelope clan establish the freshwater cisterns. The village's guardian beings—mountain lion, bear, green frog, and snake—are assigned their corner places, as if replacing the role of the Twins.

Then comes the moment for everyone to ascend "the completely kerneled long ear of corn"—a metaphoric designation for Acoma mesa itself. Arriving by the blessed trail, the medicine men receive village officials and the Antelope clan. Next come the people, clans, and societies, each assigned their specific homes or meeting places. With the people observing every ceremonial detail, the entire settling-in period consumes two days. Here they dwell for a long time: "Year after year they continued to go through their ceremonies."

With a final sentence, Edward ends his narrative, like a ribbon snipped by scissors.

"This is as far as the tradition is told."

SYMBOLS, THEMES, AND PATTERNS

Layered into Hunt's version are explanations, symbols, motifs, themes, and patterns that are found across the Pueblo Southwest. From Corn to Breath to Moisture to Centers to Cardinal Directions, key elements of their world are highlighted in various ways. When Edward Hunt told anthropologist Leslie White about corn, for example, he singled out those special ears treasured by most Pueblos, whose kernels cover their cobs to the tip. Sought out by farmers, they were ground into the sacred meal that accompanied prayers and blessings. But some of these ears were kept whole, to be clothed and adorned as the Honani fetishes that symbolized Iatiku herself, the "mother of all Indians."

Resonances of corn as a key symbol and root metaphor do not end there. According to Hunt, the Acoma tribe's male Cacique, its spiritual leader chosen from the Antelope clan and to serve for life, is regarded as Iatiku's earthly embodiment. He retains and regularly "feeds" such a fetish. Furthermore, Hunt confided, the sandstone mesa of Acoma itself is envisaged as the butt end of a giant ear of corn. So when the Cacique tells a man bringing a new bride to the Pueblo to "come on top of my head," he is conflating this key symbol's multiple meanings: staff of life, Iatiku, corn fetish, corn as mesa, and himself as an embodied summation of them all.

Hunt's stories are beset with dualities; so much comes in pairs, parallels, complementaries, opposites, or inversions. Two sisters are cocreators of the world, yet their natures and cultural preferences are diametrically opposed. While they are fighters for life, the War Twins are also destroyers. They model both how humans should defend themselves as warriors and how to protect themselves against the consequences of doing so, with rites that honor their victims' scalps in order to avoid being haunted by them.

The gods of the dependable seasons are regulators; they lack initiative, are unrepresented in Pueblo dances, and remain largely aloof from human life. But the Katsinas are controllers of uncertain weather, willful intercessors and recipients of human requests, and interact in community life. Male and female roles in the culture are distinct and separate, yet they are as complementary as those opposing seasons and their supernaturals: the summer Katsinas and the winter Kopishtaiya. For the people to survive, agriculture—the production of life—must be coupled with hunting—the taking of life.

These pairings are opposed by separations that mark what French scholar Lucien Sebag highlights as the Hunt narrative's five "crisis" moments. First is the separation between the sacred female pair and their male, godlike creator, which is followed by the second, a rift between the sisters. Third is the divorce between human beings and their "mother," which leads to the fourth, the bloody rupture between humans and their Katsina spirits. Last comes the break between humans and their War Twin protectors, which leaves the Acoma people on their own. This sequence of abandonments and closures by which a community individuates bears inescapable resemblance to the process by which human beings bid farewell to their protectors along their stages of growth toward adulthood.

Directional actions carry symbolic meaning. In Hunt's account, we encounter three movements. The first follows a vertical axis. Like corn plants whose growth strains upward, the first "humans" (or their sacred progenitors) ascend skyward through underworld tiers, each associated with its particular color, animal, and botanical species. Upon death, this order is reversed, as deceased tribespeople are said to be "planted" back into the earth. To access the powers of their generative underworlds, Pueblo ritualists descend into kivas and stamp on boards covering little cavities that symbolize the Shipapu location from whence humans first emerged. In the myth's middle section, movement along this axis continues, as Spider Woman enables the War Twins to ascend to their Father Sun's realm, where he tests them before granting their superhuman fighting skills.

A second movement is the order by which earthly features, notably the directional mountains, are created—north, west, south, east. As with the primordial actions in the myth, this counterclockwise sequence is second nature to today's Acoma people. By dance movements and physical gestures, song verses, prayerful invocations, and indrawn and exhaled breaths, the spiritual powers of these directions are always addressed in this order.

Third is the more historical, horizontal movement of migratory peoples from north to south. As the myth's third section has the emergent Acomans leaving their original Shipapu site of Emergence, they embark on their stop-and-start migration toward this "center of the universe." Here an "actual" geography takes over. Their progress is less a straight line between points than a centripetal movement, a spiraling ever inward until the slow-learning, long-suffering people gain sufficient maturity to earn their predestined homeland.

Almost in evolutionary and hierarchical sequence, the myth gradually introduces characters and creative actions that eventually come into dramatic interplay. Periodically we are given what folklorists call "explanatory motifs" that inform us how the magpie gained its coloring, why locusts are reborn underground, when pottery was invented, and so forth. Where ritual details may seem tiresome, readers must not forget that this myth is providing formulaic instructions for achieving outcomes that often defy nature's normal course (making snow fall in July), surpass ordinary human abilities (restoring the near dead to life), or conquer evil powers (identifying and killing a witch).

Other places where a reader's interest may flag are the slowed-down, close-up episodes in part 3, where the people are forced to address the apparent inability of humans and spirits to coexist. We might describe the eventual solution as an "enacted transformation," in which humans temporarily take on the powers and personalities of Katsinas. In the myth's most remarkable example of human creativity, we witness a culture inventing a dramaturgical strategy for restoring harmony with the spirit world, without whose assistance, in their uncertain environment, they will surely perish.

Peppering Hunt's version are inferences about proper social behavior, making the document a guidebook for what one might call the "Tao of Acoma." Rules about hunting are especially picky; one must feed, water, and adorn dead animals so their spirits will continue to give themselves to hunters. Similarly, one must respect one's dead enemies, lest their ghosts come back to haunt their killers. Nor must one ever ridicule the rain-bringing Katsinas. The older sacred sister's character and conduct is suggested as less than desirable; one must be generous, soft-spoken, and gentle with crops. The myth censures the disrespectful younger gamblers in the kiva, whose vulgarities toward women; their creator mother, Iatiku; and the Katsinas wreak havoc.

Linked to the version's admiration for the "common man" is

its diminished emphasis on any particular culture hero. What superheroes we have are the War Twins. But once they have cleared the land of monsters, their aggressive tendencies are deemed immoderate, generally a negative in Pueblo society. It is as if the communal ethos of the Pueblo world, with its anxieties about the polluting consequences of bloodletting, turns exploits that might otherwise arouse admiration into causes for anxiety. Violence may be necessary, but its destructive energies must never get out of hand. In a pinch, let "the people" become their own collective hero. Might Edward Hunt, a man banished from Acoma by its conservative elders, be making a personal case in the myth by setting up a comparison between the less effective office of the village Antelope Chief and the successful efforts of a modest, noninterfering "common man"?

Similarly is the Trickster figure brought under society's thumb. The first Koshari, or sacred clown—who was different from other people because, in Hunt's beguiling phrase, "he knew something about himself"—is created as a Delight Maker whose function and latitude is circumscribed. This is no antisocial agent of rampant disorder, as one finds in the Coyote trickster of neighboring tribes. The Acoma clown joins a ceremonial brotherhood and is entrusted with the tribe's most sacred teachings. His inversions of acceptable behavior take place on prescribed occasions and under clear guidelines. No matter how outrageous, no person or value is ever threatened by his burlesques. Indeed, the delight and relief everyone feels at clown performances may stem from how they allow onlookers to vicariously blow off steam over their society's behavioral strictures while simultaneously reinforcing Acoma's core values.

Hunt's version closes with the ancestors of today's Acoma people starting to live out their myth's directives and implications on their own. His story has let their cultural ethos come into being before our eyes. We have witnessed Acoma's physical world grow out to the four directions, its philosophical and moral structures come into focus, its people maturing as they explore and humanize their new world.

At the end, their former relationship with the spirits has been replaced by a divinely sanctioned but humanly created connection that requires participatory maintenance, in the form of ritual actions and proper behavior, in order to endure. Through sacred theater and impersonation, humans can *half* become the Katsinas, so as to secure their blessings. To control the weather in their favor, these masked performers can safely visit and dance and help their people through transitional moments in the year. To remind themselves of the costs of disrespecting the spirits and any humans they have killed in battle, every five years they can dramatize that terrible war and the ensuing scalp ceremony that have been so vividly recalled in this myth. The narrative has bequeathed to its Acoma people the codes of proper behavior and correct ritual so they may perpetuate their particular existence. This explains the seriousness of the Pueblo need to keep their key ceremonies and kiva practices from the eyes of outsiders, lest their powers drain away. And while these powers are initially designed for members only, they believe that their benefits extend to the entire world.

It is not easy for a culture to arrive at an integrated sense of itself. People must make their ecological surroundings comprehensible and meaningful. They must work out the kinks and contradictions born of their evolving premises. They must invent corrective devices to the negative sides of human nature and establish a moral code in accord with their cosmological principles. They must do all this generally and specifically, and they must leave room for human beings to enjoy their lives. To preserve a sense of equality, they must also disperse the knowledge of how all this works throughout the community, even if some are entitled to know what the uninitiated are not.

What Edward Hunt provided in the nation's capital was his summarizing version of a narrative that, seen from today's perspective, supported Acoma's claim of an endurable identity in the contemporary arena. By the time his ancestors installed themselves on their home mesa in western New Mexico, they had "suffered into knowledge," as the playwright Aeschylus once put it. They had earned the tools to face the future. Edward had preserved the story of how a new ethnicity joined the world's collection of distinctive small-scale societies.

PREPARING THIS EDITION

Of the dozen or so published examples of Pueblo Indian creation stories, mostly collected by anthropologists and folklorists over the past century or more, this version of the Acoma Pueblo origin myth is among the most complete ever consigned to print. It took fourteen years before it appeared, and then few noticed. It was published in the thick of World War II, drably and inexpensively released like any other official document, and distributed via the U.S. Government Printing Office's mailing list. One of its own editors had to write its first review. It would take another fifteen years before scholars and anthologizers began to appreciate its culturally bounteous and densely structured contents. Since then, it has been widely analyzed and excerpted. French anthropologist Lucien Sebag made it the centerpiece of a book-length study. Pueblo scholar Alfonso Ortiz featured it in his anthology of American Indian literature. Archaeologist Stephen H. Lekson saw it as supporting his ideas about Ancestral Pueblo migrations. Today it is recognized as one of the major contributions to American Indian mythology.

It may have been John Peabody Harrington, the eccentric genius of American Indian linguistics, who had previously met the Edward Hunt family out West and gave them entrée to the Smithsonian. However it transpired, in late August 1928, the Hunt entourage found itself at the Smithsonian Castle, in the second-floor office of Matthew W. Stirling, the brand-new "chief" of the Smithsonian's Bureau of American Ethnology.

A modest man, Stirling would have been first to admit he was not prepared for this assignment. One imagines he wished his predecessor, the southwestern ethnographer Jesse Walter Fewkes, were on deck. Not a linguist, folklorist, or ethnographer, Stirling had replaced the ailing Fewkes only weeks earlier and would hold the post for another thirty years. But he was an archaeologist, untrained at eliciting information from the living. He had excavated Indian sites in California, North Dakota, and Florida; his scholarly renown would come ten years later when *National Geographic* reported his dramatic find of huge stone heads carved by the ancient Olmecs of southwestern Veracruz.

For now, Stirling could count on ethnographic colleagues who regularly sought out native informants like the Hunts. This was the tail end of what has been described as the Smithsonian's "Golden Age of Anthropology," when documenting Indian cultures remained a priority. As the manuscript was prepared, some of the discipline's leading lights would contribute to its editing process.

No sooner did the Hunts sit down to work than they met another recent arrival to the Smithsonian. C. Daryll Forde was a twenty-six-year-old new PhD in prehistoric archaeology from University College, London. Author of a recent book on ancient seamanship and destined to become a leading Africanist, Forde was just starting a two-year Commonwealth postgraduate fellowship. Thrilled to meet real Indians while gearing up for his American field trip, he was easily recruited to transcribe in longhand Hunt's early sessions (episodes one through twenty), which Stirling let him add to his résumé through separate publication in a British folklore journal. When Stirling compiled the entire manuscript, he patched Forde's material into its opening section.

Before narrating his people's genesis, Hunt explained that "the entire account should be given in its proper sequence, just as it was taught to him during his period of initiation as a young man." Later in the storytelling, however, he was more precise and pluralistic about his actual training: "The tradition is told and taught when a man is being initiated into one of the societies." But personal circumstances had seen Edward initiated into more of them than was customary for any single Acoma man. So he seems to have sequenced a number of these various induction stories, each with its separate mythic episodes of origin, into this continuous epic.

For example, he also told Stirling, "During the 4-day period when the Chaianyi [medicine men] are setting up the altar, they tell it. The songs contain information also." Then he clarified how: "Besides, in preparing for a ceremony, that part of the tradition which they may relate is told." As an example, when Edward told of the arrival of winter Katsina, he explained, "Before the Kopishtaiya come, when the men are getting ready for them, they tell in the kiva the part [of the myth] they are going to enact. Thus they will be thoroughly familiar with the spirit and details of the ceremony." At another point, however, clarifying the importance of the Koshari Society (of which he was an initiated member), he explained how they were "the group of sacred clowns to whom theoretically all religious secrets are divulged."

These are Edward's only hints about any syntheses he was imposing on his material. Even though Stirling was new to Pueblo thought and unacquainted with their society's dispersal of cultural knowledge throughout these various groups, he sensed that "the sequential and comprehensive character of this version has given fresh meaning to various concepts and rituals of Keresan religion."

Hunt had already described some of his initiatory experiences to photographer Edward S. Curtis' hired fieldworker, Charles Strong, in 1909, and with ethnographer Leslie A. White, in 1926. Among his people, Hunt told Stirling, the narrative belonged to a genre known as *gutti'amunish wupe'ta'ni* in Keresan, which he translated as "origin tradition—by passing word from one to another."

As Stirling described their stop-and-start process, he noticed that "the tradition is couched in archaic language so that in many places the younger interpreters [Henry Wayne and Wilbert Hunt] were unable to translate and the elderly informant would have to explain in modern Acoma phraseology. This may account in part for certain obvious paraphrases of Pueblo or even of merely Indian ways of speaking. Other paraphrases may have been made for the benefit of the white man or as interpretation of Acoma religion by one who is an exceptionally good [Christian] and no longer a

participant in the ceremonial life of Acoma." As Stirling
grew impressed with the narrative's significance, it became
clear how "with this myth, according to Acoma ideology,
everything in the culture must harmonize. When new practices are adopted, there is an attempt to fit them into the
general scheme."

We presume Hunt began with phrases, which his son
Henry Wayne patiently translated into English sentences.
Watching, listening, and hurriedly writing down Henry's
translation, Stirling was struck that although the old man
was an avowed Protestant, "he apparently put himself completely into the spirit of the pagan beliefs at the time he was
recounting the narrative . . ." Periodically, Stirling may have
broken in with a question, as parenthetical comments in the
original text seem to indicate where Hunt is responding to
interruptions or volunteering asides and clarifications.

As if to underscore the narrative's authority to provide li-
turgical scripts for the proper conduct of initiations, curing
rituals, and group ceremonies so they can work their magic—
making rain, healing the sick, protecting tribal members,
staving off ghosts and witches—Stirling observed that at moments Hunt "gave what seemed to be undoubted evidence of
hesitancy and even fear in recounting certain passages."

This caution was probably because creation narratives were
rarely just *about* primordial events. Like many sacred texts, in
mysterious ways they embodied their generative powers. Reca-
pitulations in the forms of uttered words and ritual actions
perpetuated the creative forces and cultural processes of which
they spoke. At the same time, Stirling noted how Hunt took
pains "to differentiate between contemporary practice and
what was given in the tradition. Frequently after his dictation
when I would question him to bring out concrete instances, he
would say, 'It is not done so anymore.'"

Regrettable in this entire process were a number of oversights. First and greatest was Stirling's failure to record or
transcribe Hunt's narration in the Acoma dialect of his Keresan language. Neither a Pueblo linguist nor a cultural an-

thropologist, Stirling did his best, writing as rapidly in English as possible to keep up with Henry's similarly untrained translation, which he was doing in his head. But as linguistic anthropologist Dennis Tedlock, a leading scholar of Pueblo Indian sacred texts, argues, "Where style is concerned, just about anything collected by the old written dictation method is nearly worthless." Without training in orthographic methods for capturing the original language and producing an interlinear translation, which would include all repetitions and songs and the original flow of narration prior to breaking into shorter, choppier English sentences, most opportunities for any subsequent revelations about Acoman oral genres, rhetorical strategies, or deeper glosses of key concepts were lost.

Second, the song texts recorded during this time were not reincorporated into the text, where they functioned as more than adornment. By lending incantation, repetition, and vocal range to prayers and blessings, songs brought these mythic events *into the present*, much as they enabled the story's events to take place as they originally had at the dawn of creation. When anthropologist Ruth Benedict was collecting similar material at Zuni Pueblo in the summer of 1925, for instance, she praised her informant: "Nick is invaluable—if I could only take his 'singsongs' in text!" Benedict went on to describe how he "told me the emergence story with fire in his eye yesterday through twenty-two repetitions of the same episode in twenty-two 'sacred' songs. He'd tried to skip but habit was too strong."

One can imagine Hunt similarly incapable of reciting the myth without punctuating it with the songs and repetitious verses that activated the channeling of the myth's powers. Notably in part 1, where Iatiku gives life in such fixed order to key features of Acoma ecology and sociology, the verses energized the creative processes. As early ethnographer Washington Matthews wrote of Navajo sacred song sequences, here was an example where "myth is the key . . . Few songs except extemporaneous compositions exist independently of myth." Later these very same songs—heard at name givings, religious initiations and ceremonies, and critical moments in the agricultural cycle—rang out again so as to re-access their ancient potency.

Like Benedict's Zuni friend, Hunt probably exercised some sort of textual triage for the sake of the unfamiliar cause at hand, which was getting the narrative down on paper instead of re-creating ceremonial instructions for efficacious purposes. So songs were referred to but not included, prayers were mentioned but their multiday repetitions were ignored, and only an outline of ritual actions was described. Still, Hunt may have felt a twinge of unease at brokering not only a conversion from the oral to the written, but a transition from the myth's functional venues to this new archival context. Yet his frequent citing of songs underscores the mysterious, essential link between poetic expressions and real life. "Song at the very beginning was experience," wrote Acoma poet Simon Ortiz. "There was no division between experience and expression . . . The purpose of the song is first of all to do things well, the way that they're supposed to be done . . . The context in which the song is sung or that a prayer song makes possible is what makes a song substantial, gives it the quality of realness."

A third drawback was the absence of documentation on Hunt's performative or "paralinguistic" accompaniment to his spoken narration. What gestures he made, what facial expressions, where he slowed down, spoke loudly, whispered, or mimicked various participants—all that was lost. "Cut off from their performance context," laments folklorist Elaine Jahner of so many Indian texts collected over the late nineteenth and early twentieth centuries, "they are like the dry bones of skeletons. They show us only outlines, yet these are precious because they are all we have to tell us how tales were adapted as cultures faced revolutionary change."

Occasionally, father and son conferred over difficult passages, unfamiliar rituals, or ceremonial or archaic words. But apart from Stirling's idea to put a few of these "asides" in parentheses, typographical conventions such as brackets, italics, double columns, or marginal notations for documenting the "total performance" of such sessions were nonexistent in those years. I have either bled them into this edition or omitted them as redundant or nonessential. Whenever Hunt underscored that some esoteric practice was still extant, out of respect for contemporary Pueblo sensitivities I have not included them. To appreciate what was missed in this process, the scholar of traditional American Indian literatures Karl Kroeber reminds us of the customary settings for listener-narrator interaction during such oral performances in their traditional contexts: "The Indian audience listened very carefully to each teller's particular vocal inflections, verbal innovations, rhetorical omissions and additions, shifts in the order of events, modifications of character, and so forth, because these performative qualities endowed the old story with its special contemporary relevance."

Nor did Stirling provide details as to how the text's complementary songs and pictures were actually recorded. Presumably Hunt also interrupted his narration so he could direct his son Henry in correctly rendering the drawings and watercolors that illustrated the ceremonial regalia, altarpieces, and Katsina masks he mentioned in the myth. More intrinsic to the story line were those songs that punctuated the text. When Stirling separated them out, he left no "stage directions" about how they were originally sung. Altogether, nearly seventy songs were collected, sung by Philip Sanchez, and recorded on wax cylinders by Anthony Wilding, Stirling's assistant.

During the eight or nine weeks of interviews, Stirling put his pencil to 189 lined yellow pages. Once this transcription phase was done, the task of editing and annotating could begin. But that waited for nearly a decade while the manuscript languished in Stirling's files. In the spring of 1937, Leslie A. White, an anthropologist who had already written his foundational study of Acoma for the Smithsonian, *The Acoma Indians*, asked Stirling about the manuscript's present state. A year later, White began preparing its largely linguistic footnotes, with help from Elsie Clews Parsons, the independently wealthy and prolific doyenne of Pueblo Indian studies. Work on the song texts was handed out to Parsons' famous mentor, Franz Boas, who was acquainted with Keresan linguistic materials from his former work at Laguna Pueblo.

It was natural for Stirling to turn to White. As a University of Chicago graduate student in anthropology, White had made his first field trip to Acoma in the summer of 1926, when he worked closely with Edward Hunt, then living at Santa Ana Pueblo. "All the material we recorded has been annotated and generally edited by Dr. Leslie A. White," acknowledged Stirling in the original publication, "who for many years has been a student of the Keres."

Stirling also offered special thanks "to the late Dr. Elsie Clews Parsons, who took part in the editing." Not much happened in southwestern Indian scholarship without Parsons' critical review, scholarly approval, and, customarily, financial support. An heiress, early feminist, fearless ethnographer, and published author who was smitten by the anthropology courses she took under Boas at New York's Columbia University, Parsons amended Stirling's and Henry's sentences for clarity and strengthened White's commentary.

From this postnarration process, Hunt the narrator was excluded. Once he was back in New Mexico after the original narrating sessions of 1928, it was as if he had dropped his birthright into a well. He wasn't consulted for additions or double-checking. He was given no indication about when, if, or how the material would appear in print. Fourteen years later, on December 3, 1942, thirty-five hundred copies of the finished, edited version were published at a cost of nearly two thousand dollars, with two strikes against any wide response. For one, the drab green cover on its 123 pages looked more like that of a government seed catalog than a Native American equivalent to the Old Testament. Lacking a public relations office, the Bureau of American Ethnology sent no publication list to bookstores. And besides, the nation had no sooner emerged from the Depression than it was embroiled in a world war. Young scholars were now soldiers overseas. Who but a few specialists had time for such an obscure document?

For nearly two decades, the publication went largely un-noticed. Yet it was precisely the mine of cultural riches for which the French anthropological philosopher Claude Lévi-Strauss searched throughout his academic career. After convening research seminars at L'École des Hautes Études in 1951 to analyze New World myths, Lévi-Strauss waited a while to tackle the Pueblo Indian material. But during his 1961–63 sessions, he assigned Lucien Sebag, a Tunisian-born ardent practitioner of his system of structural analysis, to scrutinize this and other Keresan versions. In Sebag's posthumous 485-page book-length analysis, he nicely summarized Hunt's material: "The text forms an homogeneous whole which begins with the creation of the world and finishes with the settlement of the Acomas at the center of the world. Its coherence is total, and one does not note contradictions between the diverse parts of the myth. This is the greatest Keresan myth that has reached us, and it will constitute the center of our research."

When scholars and anthologizers explored American Indians and world mythology a few decades later, they rediscovered the unique window offered by this publication into Pueblo Indian rituals, metaphysics, and ethics.

A NOTE ON THIS TEXT

Thirty years ago, while working on a book on American Indian architecture, I was canvassing American Indian creation stories for references to the cosmological meanings encoded in native buildings. In a Smithsonian Institution bulletin, I ran across this anonymously authored account of Acoma's sacred "mother of all Indians," Iatiku, magically creating their first houses, plaza, kivas, and sacred places. After quoting from that work and citing it a second time for a subsequent book exclusively on the architecture of Acoma Pueblo, I remained curious about its narrator. That led me into a quarter-century investigation of the remarkable life of Edward Proctor Hunt, which is now the core of *How the World Moves: The Odyssey of an American Indian Family*, a biographical work on the man, his family, and their times.

But I also thought the origin myth deserved a wider readership and a treatment that provided its background, profiled its narrator, and made this big story more accessible. To that end, I conducted a sentence-by-sentence examination of the 1942 edition; reviewed official correspondence and papers associated with this Bulletin 135 of the Bureau of American Ethnology at the Smithsonian's National Anthropological Archives; and located Stirling's original, handwritten transcript in the Elsie Clews Parsons papers at Philadelphia's American Philosophical Society (Mss. no. 4846).

From this research it became unfortunately clear that from a contemporary scholar's perspective, the three oversights of the original sessions—failures to record it in the native tongue; to incorporate song texts in their proper places; and to document Edward's storytelling pace, tone, and gestures—had weakened that first publication. But for a general readership, the story remained valuable and warranted another edition.

I realized that a portion of the original narration, relating the birth and exploits of the War Twins, was relegated to an appendix, along with Hunt's asides on installing Acoma tribal officers and initiating members of its Katsina and Koshari societies. I restored the Twins section to its sequentially appropriate middle place, creating a tripartite narrative and letting that section serve as the bridge between the more mythical and more historical parts of the story.

After reading the work numerous times, I also felt that Stirling's paragraphing was cumbersome. This led me to imagine ways to open up his text while retaining its integrity. Retyping the entire work three times, in the process of reparagraphing, I discovered subtle breaks or "breathers" between discrete actions. All told, I discerned eighty-two of these "scenes," which proved of more or less equal length. Since Stirling kept no day-to-day log of the original storytelling process, I have no evidence whether this conformed to the pace of the original storytelling and translating. But the total time might have fit into eight or so five-day weeks of continuous narration, with each of these separate scenes possibly completed on a given morning and afternoon. After redrafting this restored, three-part version, between these scenes I then interspersed brief present-tense summaries to help readers follow the drama.

My examination of texts of the myth's songs recorded at the Smithsonian and their mentions in the actual myth made me confident about reinserting at least a few at their proper place in the document. I attempted this so as to provide readers with something of the flavor of the performative dimension of the stories Hunt was stringing together.

In my last review, I worked on the sentences with care, omitting only a few to eliminate redundancies, occasionally splitting them into two, at times clarifying a word or finding a synonym when I encountered a term that was confusing or that I suspected present-day Indians might dislike, such as rejecting "costume" in favor of "outfit" or "regalia." To further respect contemporary Pueblo concerns about publishing visual images of sensitive cultural features, I have omitted all of Henry's thirty-six illustrations and the historical photographs, maps, and drawings that were included in the original publication. The written account should be sufficient for the reader's imagination.

Narratives of great magnitude like the Acoma creation story, lacking ultimate authors and going back to unknowable beginnings, are inexhaustible. Their multiple versions always yield new meanings; Edward's contribution is only one of them. Attempting to "get to the bottom" of any of them is futile and presumptuous. No matter how directed and developed by an individual narrator, they remain repositories of a collective imagination and are driven by cultural survival. One of humankind's greatest artistic productions, they are at once specific, universal, and essential.

PETER NABOKOV

The Origin Myth of
Acoma Pueblo

PART ONE

IATIKU'S WORLD

I.

At the underworld place called Shipapu, the first two girls are born and raised. A spirit named Tsichtinako teaches them to talk.

In the beginning two female human beings were born. They were born underground at a place called Shipapu. As they grew up, they began to be aware of each other. There was no light and they could only feel each other. Being in the dark they grew slowly.

After they had grown considerably, a spirit whom they afterward called Tsichtinako spoke to them. They found that this spirit would give them nourishment. After they were large enough to think for themselves they spoke to the spirit when it came to them one day. They asked it to make itself known to them and to say whether it was male or female. But the spirit would only reply that it was not allowed to meet with them.

They asked why they were living in the dark without knowing each other by name. The spirit answered that they were under the earth. They should be patient and wait until everything was ready for them to go up into the light.

So they waited a long time. As they grew they learned their language from Tsichtinako.

2.

The girls are given baskets containing seeds and fetishes. They plant the seeds, and the fastest-growing tree breaks into the light above.

When all was ready, they found a present from Tsichtinako. It was two baskets containing seeds and little images of all the different animals that would be in the world. The spirit said that they were sent by their father. They wanted to know, who was meant by their father? Tsichtinako replied that his name was Uchtsiti and that he wished them to take their baskets out into the light, when the time came.

Tsichtinako said, "You'll find the seeds of four different kinds of pine trees in your baskets. You're to plant them and use the trees to climb up into the light." They could not see the things in their baskets. But feeling each object in turn, they asked, "Is this it?" until all the seeds were found.

Then they planted the seeds as Tsichtinako had instructed.

All of them sprouted. But in the darkness the trees grew slowly. During this long time the two sisters waited and became anxious to reach the light. For many years they slept. As they had no use for eyes, each time they awoke they felt the trees to see how they were growing.

One tree grew faster than the others. After a long time it pushed a hole through the earth for them and let in a little light. When this happened, the others stopped growing, at their various heights.

3.

First the badger and then the locust are told to en-
large and smoothen this opening to the earth above.
They are sent to see what it is like up there.

The hole made by the tree was not large enough for the girls
to pass through. So Tsichtinako advised them to look again
in their baskets for the image of an animal called Badger.
They should tell it to become alive. It did and exclaimed,
"A'uha! Why have you given me life?"

They told Badger not to be afraid or worry about coming
alive. "We've brought you to life because you'll be useful."

Again Tsichtinako spoke to the girls, instructing them to
tell Badger to climb the pine tree and open a hole large
enough for them to crawl through. They cautioned him not
to continue into the light, but to return once the hole was
finished. Badger went up the tree and dug a bigger hole. He
came back and said that his work was done.

They thanked him. "As a reward you'll come up with us
to the light and thereafter you'll live happily," they said.
"You'll always know how to dig and your home will be in
the ground where you'll neither be too hot or too cold."

Now Tsichtinako told them to look in the basket for Locust. They were to give him life and ask him to smooth the
hole by plastering it. They should warn him to return when he
was done. This they did, and Locust smoothed the hole. But
instead of coming back, he briefly went out into the light.

When Locust returned and reported that his work was
over, the girls asked if he had gone out. At first Locust de-
nied it. Every time he was asked he said no. Finally the
fourth time he admitted that he had. When they asked what
it was like out there he said that it was just laid out flat.

"From now on you'll be known as Locust," they said.

"You'll also come up with us. But you'll be punished for disobedience by only being allowed out for a short time. Your home will be in the ground and you'll have to return when the weather is bad. Soon you'll die, but you'll be reborn each season."

4.

Carrying their baskets of seeds, animal effigies, and offerings, the two girls climb up and onto the soft earth. They greet the four directions and the sun. They are named Iatiku and Nautsiti.

As the hole let light into where the two sisters were, Tsichtinako said it was time for them to go up and out. "You can take your baskets with you. In them you'll find pollen and sacred corn meal. When you reach the top, you'll wait for the sun to come up. That direction will be called East. With the pollen and sacred corn meal you'll pray to the Sun. You'll thank the Sun for bringing you to light. You'll ask for long life and happiness and for success in the purpose for which you were created."

Tsichtinako taught them the prayers and the creation song, which they were to sing.

Already, a long time ago,
From the underworld,
Southward they came.
With life, with crops,
Carrying useful things, they came.
Already, a long time ago,
From the underworld,
Southward they came.
Already, a long time ago,
From the underworld,
Southward they came.
With cloud, with fog, carrying useful things,
With these, the pure, the handsome people, were nourished.
Already, a long time ago,
From the underworld,

Southward they came.
With crops, carrying useful things, they came.
With these the common people,
Handsome and pure,
Were nourished.

All this took a long while. Finally the sisters, followed by
Badger and Locust, climbed the pine tree and went up and
into the light. Badger was strong and skillful and helped them.

On reaching the earth, they set down their baskets and
saw for the first time what they had. As they walked the earth
was soft and spongy under their feet. "This isn't ripe," they
said. They stood waiting for the sun, not knowing where it
would appear.

Gradually everything grew lighter. Finally the sun came up.
Before they began to pray, Tsichtinako told them they were
facing east and that their right side, the side their best aim was
on, would be known as South. To their left was North, and
behind, at their backs, was the direction where the sun would
go down. While underground they had already learned the
direction Down. Later, when they asked where their father
was, they were told Four Skies Above.

As they waited to pray to the Sun, the girl on the right
moved her best hand and was named Iatiku, which meant
"bringing to life." Then Tsichtinako noticed that the other
girl had more in her basket, so Tsichtinako told Iatiku to
name her thus. Iatiku called her sister Nautsiti, which meant
"more of everything in the basket."

They prayed to the Sun, as they had been taught, and sang
this creation song.

When I came out, when I came out,
Who was it that was born this morning?
It was that—the earth, the sky—
They were born this morning.
It was that—the sun, the moon—
They were born this morning.

It was that—the rainbow, the stars—
They were born this morning.
When I came out, when I came out, who was born this morning?

Their eyes hurt for they were not accustomed to the strong light.

5.

The sisters ask the Spirit why they have been created, where their father lives, and how they will survive. They experience their first night on earth.

For the first time the sisters asked Tsichtinako why they were on earth and why they were created. "I didn't make you," Tsichtinako answered. "Your father, Uchtsiti, made you. He made the world, the sun which you've seen, the sky, and many other things which you will see. But Uchtsiti says the world isn't completed as satisfactorily as he wants it. This is why he made you. You'll rule and bring to life the rest of the things he's given you in the baskets."

The sisters asked how they had come into being. "Uchtsiti first made the world," Tsichtinako answered. "He threw a clot of his own blood into space. By his power it grew and grew until it became the earth. Then Uchtsiti planted you in this. By it you were nourished as you developed. Now that you've emerged from within the earth, you'll have to provide nourishment for yourselves and I'll teach you how."

They asked where their father lived. "You'll never see your father," Tsichtinako replied. "He lives four skies above, and created you to live in this world. He's made you in the image of himself." So they asked why Tsichtinako did not become visible to them. "I don't know how to live like a human being," Tsichtinako answered. "I've been asked by Uchtsiti to look after you and teach you. I'll always guide you."

Again they asked how they were to live and if they could go back down under the ground. They were afraid of the winds and rains and their eyes were hurt by the light. Tsichtinako said that Uchtsiti would take care of all that. He would furnish them the means to keep warm and change the atmosphere so they would get used to it.

When it grew dark at the end of the first day they became

afraid, for they had not realized that the sun would set. They thought Tsichtinako had betrayed them. "Tsichtinako! Tsichtinako! You told us we were to come into the light," they cried. "Why is it dark?"

Tsichtinako explained, "This is the way it'll always be. The sun will go down and the next day it'll come up anew in the east. When it's dark you're to rest, and sleep as you slept before when everything was dark."

They were satisfied and slept.

6.

To distinguish the sisters from each other, the Spirit gives them different clans, complexions, and ways of thinking.

The girls rose to meet the sun and prayed to it as they had been told. They were happy when it rose again, for then they were warm and their faith in Tsichtinako was restored.

Tsichtinako said to them, "Now that you've your names, you'll pray with them and with your clan names so that the Sun will know you and recognize you." Tsichtinako asked which clan Nautsiti wished to belong to. "I wish to see the sun," she answered. "That is the clan I'll be, the Sun clan."

The spirit told her to ask her sister what clan she wanted. Iatiku thought for a long time. Finally she noticed that her basket only contained the seed from which sacred meal was made. "With this name I shall be proud," she thought, "for it's been chosen for nourishment and it's sacred." So she said, "I'll be Corn clan."

They waited for the sun to come up again. When it appeared, Tsichtinako had them sing the first song once more and pray. She told them not to forget to say their names and clans in starting their prayer. After that they were to sing the second song.

The sun was too bright for Iatiku and hurt her eyes. She wondered if Nautsiti's eyes hurt, too. So she put her head down sideways and let her hair shade her face. She looked at Nautsiti. "Iatiku, the sun hasn't appeared for you," Tsichtinako said. "Look at Nautsiti, see how strongly the light is striking her. Notice how white she looks." Although Iatiku turned to the sun, it did not make her as white as Nautsiti. Iatiku's mind was slowed up, but Nautsiti's mind was fast.

Both of them remembered everything and behaved as they were taught.

7.

*The sisters are given instructions for praying to the
four directions and for planting the seeds from
their baskets. First they plant the corn.*

When they completed their prayers to the sun, Tsichtinako
said, "You've done everything well and now you're to take up
your baskets. You must look to the north, west, south, and
east, for now you're to pray to the Earth to accept the things
in the basket and give them life. First you must pray to the
north, at the same time raise your baskets in that direction.
Then do the same to the west, south, and east." They did as
told and did it well. Tsichtinako said to them, "From now on
you'll rule in every direction—north, west, south, and east."

They questioned Tsichtinako again so as to understand
more clearly why they were given the baskets and their contents. "Everything in the baskets is to be created by your
word," Tsichtinako explained. "You're made in the image
of Uchtsiti and your word will be as powerful as his word.
He's created you to help him complete the world. You're to
plant the seeds of different plants, to be used when they are
needed. I'll always be ready to point out to you the various
plants and animals."

The sisters did not realize that they were not taking food.
They did not understand when Tsichtinako told them they
should plant seeds for nourishment. But they were ready to
do as she said. First she had them plant that which would
maintain life—grains of corn.

"When this plant grows," said Tsichtinako, "it'll produce
a part which I'll point out to you. This will be taken as
food." Everything in the basket was in pairs, and the sisters
planted two of each kind of corn.

The corn grew slowly. So Tsichtinako told them to grow a
plant which is the first to sprout in the spring. It is gray with

a small white flower and dies quickly. That would transmit its power of early ripening to the corn.

The sisters were interested in the corn, and watched it grow every day. When their first plants were coming up they sang this song.

Dear, dear corn maiden,
You stand in the middle of the garden, do you not?
We sing for you, this is what we have said.
Dear, dear vine-plant maiden,
You have spread out your arms in the middle of the garden.
We are making an offering to you.
This is what we have sung.
Up, up, the corn plant maiden, the vine-plant maiden,
Begin to come out.
There the corn plant maiden, the vine-plant maiden,
Begin to bear grains.

Tsichtinako showed them where the corn pollen came. "When the pollen is plentiful," she said, "you'll gather it. With pollen and corn meal you'll pray to the rising sun every morning." This they always did, but sometimes Nautsiti was a little lazy.

After some time the corn ripened. Tsichtinako told them to watch it and gather some. They saw that the corn was hard and picked four ears. Iatiku pulled off two carefully without hurting the plant. But Nautsiti jerked hers free. Iatiku noticed this and cautioned her sister not to ruin the plants.

8.

The girls receive the gift of fire. With it they roast the corn. Using salt, they eat for the first time and thank the Spirit.

They brought the ears of corn to Tsichtinako and said, "We've brought the corn. It is ripe." Tsichtinako agreed, and explained that when cooked the ears would be their food. They did not understand and asked what they would cook with. Tsichtinako said that Uchtsiti would give them fire.

That night as they sat around they saw a red light fall from the sky. Tsichtinako told them it was fire and that they should go and get some. They asked with what, and she said with a flat rock because it was hot and they could not hold it with their hands. After getting it with a rock, they asked what next to do. They were told to go to a pine tree they had planted and break off some branches and put them in the fire.

They went and broke them off. Returning to the fire, they were told to throw the twigs down. When they did this a large pile of wood suddenly appeared. Tsichtinako said that this wood would last many years, until there was time for trees to grow back. She showed them how to build the fire, and said that with its flames they would warm themselves and cook their food.

Tsichtinako taught them how to roast the corn. "When it's cooked," she explained, "you're to eat it. This will be the first time you have eaten, for you've been fasting a long time and Uchtsiti has been nourishing you. In your baskets you'll find salt to season the corn." Right away Nautsiti grabbed some corn and salt. She was the first to taste them, and exclaimed that they were good. After Nautsiti ate some she gave it to Iatiku to taste.

When both had eaten, Tsichtinako told them that this was the way they were going to live and be nourished. They were thankful and said, "You've treated us well."

9.

The salt is given life. The sisters are taught to plant tobacco and to pray with it.

The sisters wanted to know if this would be their only food. Tsichtinako said, "No, you've other things in your baskets, many seeds and images of animals, all in pairs. Some will be taken for nourishment by you." After they had used the salt, they were told by Tsichtinako to give life to it by praying to the Earth—first in the North direction, then in the West, then in the South, and finally in the East. When they did so, salt appeared in each of those directions.

Tsichtinako instructed them to pull the husks from the ears of corn carefully and to dry them. They were also shown how to plant tobacco. When the plant matured, they were taught how to roll the leaves in pieces of corn husk and smoke it.

They were also told to place the tobacco with the pollen and corn meal. These three should always be together, and be used in making prayers.

10.

*The Spirit shows the girls how to give life to the
animal images from their baskets. After they pray,
they eat flesh for the first time.*

Now the sisters were told to give life to the first animal whose
flesh they were going to use for food. Tsichtinako named it
Kangaroo Mouse and taught them the first song to be sung
to the animals. She pointed to all the images in their baskets
and said they must sing to them so they could come alive.

> Who was first to come out?
> Who was first to come out?
> It was them,
> Forefathers of all desert pocket mice.
> They were first to come out.
> Who was first to come out?
> Who was first to come out?
> It was them,
> Forefathers of all jack rabbits.
> They were first to come out.
> Who was first to come out?
> Who was first to come out?
> It was them,
> Forefathers of all deer and mountain sheep.
> They were first to come out.
> Who was first to come out?
> Who was first to come out?
> It was them,
> Forefathers of two different kinds of elk.
> They were first to come out.
> Who was first to come out?
> Who was first to come out?
> It was them,

Forefathers of slow deer and buffalo.
They were first to come out.
Who was first to come out?
Who was first to come out?
It was them,
Forefathers of pronghorn antelope.
They were first to come out.

So they sang the song to the image. With the words, "Come to life, Kangaroo Mouse," it came to life. It asked, "Why have I come to life?" Tsichtinako told it not to ask any questions. "You're going to give life to other life," she said.

Nautsiti and Iatiku told this animal that it was going to live on the ground. "Go now and increase," they said. After the animal did so, Tsichtinako told the sisters to kill one. "Now eat the two together, the corn and the mouse, and the salt to see how it tastes." She already warned them never to let the fire go out.

They acted accordingly. They roasted their corn and the flesh of the mouse with some salt. After it was cooked, Tsichtinako told them to pray with the food, not with all of it, but with little pieces from each—corn, flesh, and salt. They did this and prayed to Uchtsiti, creator of the world, who lives up in the fourth sky.

Tsichtinako told them always to do this before eating. After this they ate. There was not much meat, but it tasted good. They did not expect the bones, but they could break them with their teeth. They liked the flesh so well that they asked Tsichtinako if they might have something larger that would have more meat.

She answered that there were other things in their baskets. So they went back to them. Tsichtinako said they would find Rat, another animal, Mole, and also Prairie Dog. "Go make these images come alive," said Tsichtinako, pointing them out according to their names. They were to do just as they had done with Kangaroo Mouse.

II.

In each of the four directions the girls are taught to plant grass seeds so the small animals will have food.

Tsichtinako told the sisters to use these animals as food. But they must tell them to live within the ground because there was still no shade on earth. "Before you give life to them," she said, "you must plant seeds for the grass which will be their food."

Tsichtinako pointed out what seeds they were to plant. They scattered them to the North, West, South, and the East. Immediately grass covered the ground.

They took the images and prayed to the cardinal points. Following Tsichtinako's instructions they gave life to all of these animals, naming each one as they came alive. When they asked why they had come to life Tsichtinako told them not to ask questions. They were to give life to other life. As before, the sisters told the animals to increase. Once this was done, they prayed with the new animals and proceeded to eat them, doing as they had done before.

The sisters were happy. They had plenty and some to spare. "It's not yet time for the larger animals to be given life," said Tsichtinako. "First the world must have enough plants and small animals to feed them."

I 2.

With the Spirit's help, the girls create the mountains of the four directions. They grow trees on their slopes—to provide logs for building houses and wild seeds and nuts to eat.

After a long while, Tsichtinako spoke to them, "What we are going to do now concerns the earth. We're going to make the mountains."

She told them to remember her words. They were to say, "North Mountain, appear in the north, and we'll always know you to be in that direction." Tsichtinako pointed out an article in the basket that she named Stone, and told the sisters to throw it to the North as they spoke those words again. When they did, a big mountain appeared in the North. Tsichtinako had them do the same thing in the West, the South, and the East.

Once this was done, Tsichtinako spoke again. "Now that you have all the mountains around you with plains, mesas, and canyons, you must make the growing things of these places."

She told them to go back to the four different kinds of trees which they had planted underground. They should take seeds from them, and they did. Following her instructions they spread some in each of the four directions, naming each of the mountains as they said, "Grow in North Mountain, grow in West Mountain, grow in South Mountain, grow in East Mountain." Tsichtinako explained, "These are going to be tall trees. From them you'll get logs. Later you'll build houses and use these."

The sisters asked if that was all that was going to grow on the mountains. "No," Tsichtinako said. "There are many other seeds left in your baskets. You have seeds of trees which are going to yield food. You'll find Piñon, a kind of Cedar, Acorn Oak, and Walnut." Again she instructed them what to do and the prayer to use. It went: "From now on, grow in this mountain and yield fruit which will be used as food. Your places are to be in the mountains. You'll grow and be useful."

When everything was done well, Tsichtinako pointed out smaller seeds left in the baskets. To each she gave a name, and told the sisters to fill the rest of the land. These seeds were planted on each of the four mountains and throughout the rest of the world.

Again Tsichtinako spoke to them. "You still have seeds in your baskets which you'll know as Wild Fruits. You'll grow these trees around you and care for them." But the sisters misunderstood. Instead of instructing the seeds to grow nearby, they named the far mountains, so that is where they grew. But there were also some that grew close by.

It is not known how long they had to wait for these things to happen, but it took a long time. The sisters noticed that the wild plants grew fast and produced much fruit. But Tsichtinako had not told them whether or not to eat them, so they left them alone.

13.

*The baskets continue to produce. They yield squash
and bean seeds, middle-size animals, game animals
for hunting, and the prey animals that hunt like people. While Nautsiti is selfish, Iatiku is generous.*

The sisters noticed that there were more seeds and images in
their baskets. They wanted to know how many kinds there
were. Tsichtinako named the other seeds which would be important Squash and Beans and said they would grow quickly
and easily. The sisters were to treat them as they had the other
seeds. When they ripened Tsichtinako pointed out the parts to
use as food.

Later Iatiku asked Tsichtinako, "What remains in my basket?" "You still have many animals," she was told. "These may
multiply and populate the mountains." As the sisters grew
larger, they required more food. Tsichtinako saw this and told
them that it was time to bring the larger animals to life.

In their baskets they would find Cottontails, Jack Rabbits, Antelope, and Water Deer, she said. They were to give
life to them and send them into the open plains. Everything
was done as before. Whenever they killed the animals for
food they should be careful to pray to their father.

Once again they asked Tsichtinako what else lay in their
baskets. "You have images of still bigger game," they were
told. "Deer, Elk, Mountain Sheep, and Bison." Iatiku wondered where these animals should live. Tsichtinako replied
that the elk and deer would go to the lower mountains, the
mountain sheep higher in the rougher places, and the bison
to the plains. They did as told and gave life to these animals.
They told them to go to these places, to live and multiply.
They tried to eat them all. The flesh was good, and they always prayed to Uchtsiti before tasting it.

More was left in Nautsiti's basket than in Iatiku's. Nautsiti was selfish and hoarded her images, but Iatiku was ready to let her seeds and images be used. She was more interested in seeing things grow. Once again they asked what remained. "You'll find Lion, Wolf, Wildcat, and Bear," Tsichtinako answered. "These are strong beasts. They're going to eat the same game you eat. Now there's enough for them."

When all these had been selected they were brought to life in the same manner as before.

14.

The sisters give life to more animals: to brightly colored birds, and to fish, water snakes, and turtles.

Again the sisters asked what was left in their baskets. "You'll find birds which fly in the air," they were told. "These birds will also use small game for their food. And you'll find the Eagles and different Hawks." As Tsichtinako pointed them out, the girls brought them to life. The birds flew into the high mountains and over the plains. They told the birds to use small game for food.

When Iatiku asked what else was in the basket, Tsichtinako pointed out smaller birds which would populate the country, each in a different region. They were given life, as with the animals before them. The birds were of many bright colors, and some were blue. Among them was Wild Turkey. They were instructed to tell it not to fly easily like the others. The sisters were to tell these birds that their food would be the different seeds on the mountains and plains. After they had been given life all these animals were sampled for food.

Iatiku wanted to know what remained in the baskets, because she found things that were thorny. Tsichtinako gave their names. They were the various cacti and were said to be good for food. But Tsichtinako explained that most of them were intended for animals to eat. All were planted as before and tried for food, and some tasted good.

When they asked what remained Tsichtinako pointed out Fish, Water Snakes, and Turtles—many kinds of each. As before, they gave life to them, and directed them to live in the water. Tsichtinako indicated several to be used for food. They tried them and found that some were good and others poor. But they offered prayers for all of them and gave thanks to Uchtsiti.

So it happened that many animals came alive in the world and all increased.

15.

A strange snake comes to life. The sisters begin to fall out, competing over who is oldest. With help from a magpie, Iatiku tricks her sister in order to win.

When Tsichtinako was instructing Iatiku and Nautsiti, she warned them to be careful in handling the baskets. For a while they were, but they became too eager to give life to what remained and grew careless. While Iatiku and Nautsiti were giving life to the snakes and fishes they dropped one image on the ground. They did not realize that this had happened, nor did Tsichtinako.

The image came to life itself, with a power of its own. The two sisters noticed a strange snake among the ones to which they had given life, but only stopped long enough to ask each other, "Did we give life to that snake?" That was all the attention they paid since it looked like the others. This was the snake that would tempt Nautsiti.

Now Nautsiti spoke to Iatiku, who had used more of the seeds and images from her basket. She wanted the chance to give life to more of her images. Iatiku replied, "I'm the older, you're younger than I." But Nautsiti said, "We should give life equally because we were created equally."

Then she wondered, "Is it true that you're older? Let's test each other! Tomorrow, when the sun rises, let's see who will have the sun rise for her first."

Iatiku was afraid that her sister would somehow get the better of her. She knew the white bird that was named Magpie. She asked it to fly on ahead to the east, where the sun would rise, without resting or eating. There it would use its wings to shade the sun from Nautsiti.

The bird was strong and skillful and flew off as told. But on the way it got hungry and passed a place where a puma had killed a deer. Although it had been instructed not to stop, it found a hole in the deer's side where the intestines were exposed. Putting its head into the gash to eat, it got blood on its back, wings, and tail. It flew on but did not notice that it was stained.

After a long time, the bird reached the east where the sun was about to rise. It spread its wings on the left side of the sun, making a shade in the direction of Nautsiti. So the sun struck Iatiku first. Straightaway she claimed to be the older. Nautsiti was angry because she had hoped to win.

Iatiku did not want her sister to know about the trick. So when the bird returned she whispered to it not to say anything. She also noticed it was dirty with blood and punished it for disobeying her. "For stopping and eating from now on you won't know how to kill your own meat," she said. "You won't be a hunter but will eat what others have killed and left. Most of the time you'll eat what is spoiled. From now on your color will be spotted, you won't be as white as you were at first."

16.

As their differences grow, Nautsiti is tempted by the snake. Impregnated by drops from the rainbow, she gives birth to twin sons. Tsichtinako is angry at being disobeyed and leaves the sisters to care for the boys on their own.

Now the sisters were thinking selfish thoughts. Nautsiti schemed to get the better of Iatiku. Often she wandered off, making plans to outdo her. But Iatiku watched and noticed everything. She saw that Nautsiti was falling away from her and not as happy as before. Iatiku tried to comfort her, and asked why she had changed.

A long time before this Tsichtinako had told them that Uchtsiti forbade them from thinking about having children. In due time other humans made in their likeness would be born to them. But one day the snake that had come to life by itself met Nautsiti. "Why are you lonely and unhappy?" it asked. "If you want to be happy, I can tell you what to do. You're the only lonely one on earth. You and your sister don't like each other. If you bore someone like yourself, you would no longer be alone. Tsichtinako wants to hold this happiness from you. Unless you do as I tell you, you'll have to wait a long time."

Nautsiti wondered how to do this. "Go to the rainbow," the serpent replied. "He'll meet you and show you what to do." Nautsiti thought she should follow this advice. Soon afterwards she was sitting alone on a rock and it rained. It was hot, the rain steamed on the ground. Nautsiti lay on her back to receive it, the dripping water entered her. This was the work of rainbow. She conceived without knowing what had happened. Some time after, Iatiku noticed that Nautsiti was pregnant. After a time she bore twin sons. Iatiku helped her sister take care of them.

When Tsichtinako returned she asked, "Why have you done this without my instructing you? Uchtsiti has forbidden it." She got angry and left. But first she said, "From now on you'll do as you see fit. I won't help you anymore because you disobeyed your father."

Instead of being sorry, the two sisters felt happier. It happened that Nautsiti disliked one of the children. So Iatiku took this one and cared for it.

17.

Iatiku rejects her sister's offer of items from her basket—domesticated animals and plants, metal, and written words. They separate for good, each taking one of the twins.

Because the sisters had committed a sin, their father, Uchtsiti, called Tsichtinako away from them. The women lived together and the boys grew up. But after a long time Nautsiti said to Iatiku, "We're no longer happy together. Let's share what we have in our baskets and separate. I still have many things. These animals in my basket, these sheep and cattle, I'll share with you. But they'll demand much care."

Iatiku said it would be too hard to look after them, and she did not want her children to have them. Nautsiti pointed out some seeds and told Iatiku to take some—they would grow wheat and vegetables. She knew that they would be hard to raise, but she wanted to share them. Iatiku did not want them for her children either.

Also in Nautsiti's basket were many metals. When she offered to share these, Iatiku refused. When Nautsiti looked deep into her basket she found "something written." Although she offered this as well, again Iatiku declined.

Then Nautsiti said, "There are still many things that are good for foods in my basket but I know they'll all require care. Why is it, sister, that you're not thankful? Why don't you take what I've offered? I'm going to leave you. We both understand that we're to increase our kind. In a long time to come we'll meet again and then you'll be wearing clothes. We'll still be sisters, for we have the same father, but I'll have the better of you. I'm leaving for the East."

Iatiku sang this song as a plea to her sister.

Nautsiti, why are you crying?
No one [over there] wants to be related to you.
No one [over there] wants you to help in offerings.
Do not cry anymore.
Come back soon.
Iatiku wants to be your relative.
Iatiku needs you to help in offerings.
Do not cry anymore.

Iatiku decided to stay where she was. So Nautsiti left, taking the child she loved with her and leaving the other with her sister.

18.

When Iatiku's nephew grows up he becomes her husband. She has many children and teaches each one to pray to the sun. After naming the first child for the Sun clan, she establishes the rest of the clans.

Nautsiti disappeared into the East, while Iatiku stayed on and grew sad. She told the boy child who remained with her, "We'll survive with everything our father has given us." For a long time they lived together. When he grew up, he became her husband and she named him Tiamunyi. Iatiku bore many children and she named the first after the clan of her sister— the Sun clan.

Now Iatiku had her own power. She did everything as she had been taught. The fourth day after her first birth she took the child to pray to the sun, just as she was taught when she first came into the light. She put some pollen and sacred corn meal into the child's hands. She taught this to every child she bore after this.

All the brothers and sisters lived together and began to increase. Iatiku was the mother and she ruled. Whenever a child was born to her, she gave it a clan name. The first clan mothers, in order of birth, were as follows: Sun clan, named because Iatiku was still grieving over Nautsiti who had named herself of the Sun clan, Sky clan, Water clan, Badger clan, Fire clan.

After naming these, she thought she would name the rest of the children after the things she'd brought to life. So in that order, the next were named: Antelope clan, Deer clan, Bear clan.

But she didn't want to give out her own name, Corn clan, as she wanted to be kept apart. So she divided the kinds of corn as follows: Red corn, Yellow corn, Blue corn, White corn.

The next clans in order were: Oak clan, Squash clan, Road-runner clan, Eagle clan, Turkey clan, Tansy Mustard clan. Later, other clans came into existence—Parrot, Snake, Buffalo, and Ant. But they were not descended from daughters of Iatiku.

19.

Abandoned by both Tsichtinako and her sister, Iatiku takes earth from her basket to create the ruling spirits of the four seasons in their mountain homes. She teaches her children how to pray to these spirits so they can survive.

Now that Tsichtinako had left her, Iatiku wished for other rulers. So she made the spirits of the seasons. There was still some earth in her basket. She gave it life in the same way as before.

First she made the spirit of Winter. To him she said, "You'll give life to everything in winter time. You're to be ugly and ferocious. You won't live with us, go away some distance. You'll live in North Mountain, and I'll give you your costume."

Next she gave life to the spirit of Spring. To him she gave an ugly costume, and sent him to West Mountain. Then she made the Summer spirit and sent him to South Mountain. Finally she gave life to the spirit of Fall, and sent him to East Mountain.

All these creatures were ugly and not in the likeness of her children. "Now that I've placed strong rulers in every direction," she thought, "they'll order the earth in turn." She told them all where to work and how.

The spirit of Winter was to bring snow. The spirit of Spring would warm up the world. The spirit of Summer would heat it, giving life to vegetation. The spirit of Fall would not like the smell of plants and fruits and would get rid of their odor by clearing the world of them.

Iatiku told her children that they were to depend on these spirits, and pray to them in their respective directions—for moisture, warmth, ripening, and frost. She taught them how to make their prayers, explaining that each spirit would require preferred prayers and prayer sticks before they responded.

20.

Iatiku creates the spirits called Katsinas. They include the handsome Chief Katsina and summer spirit, the ferocious Winter Katsina, and the Messenger Katsina. To each she gives their distinctive mask and dress. Finally she gives life to two more spirits, a couple who will rule the winter clouds.

When this was done, Iatiku gave life to the other spirits she was going to believe in. With dirt from her basket she gave life to the Katsinas. The first she named Tsitsanits (no female was made for this first one). The others she created male and female. She named Kuashtoch ("Sticking Up") from the feathers on one side of the head. The next, Kuapichani ("Divided"), was named because one side of his face is yellow and the other red. Then she made other Katsinas: Duck, Jemez, Nawish ("Farmer"), Bear, Kakuipe, Messenger, Hopi, Ahote, and Chayoka, who is a great hunter.

She called Tsitsanits to her. "I'm going to give you your outfit," she said. "You're handsome, but you'll have a mask which will make you appear different from humans." Like all the others, she fashioned it from buffalo skin so that it fit him. Coloring it from different earths she put different feathers on it. After putting it on his head she wrapped a wildcat skin around his neck, painted his body, and gave him a skirt, belt, and moccasins. Around each wrist she tied cords, and dyed buffalo skins on his arms. On his calves she bound spruce branches.

When she was done Iatiku said to Tsitsanits, "You see that I've created many other spirits and appointed you as their ruler. You'll initiate the rest." To perform this ritual she gave him blades of yucca plant.

Then Iatiku took more dirt from the basket and gave life to Kopishtaiya and his wife. "You look ferocious," she told them. "So you'll have to live in a different place."

2 1 .

For people to receive blessings from these spirits, Iatiku begins the practice of prayer stick offerings. She sends the Katsinas to their new home under a lake and explains how human beings and Katsinas will now have lives that depend on each other.

The first Katsina named Tsitsanits asked Iatiku where he was going to live, in what direction, what his work would be, and who would govern him. "Take the Katsinas with you to Wenimats, west and south of here," she told him. This was at a lake with weeds growing in it, and under it lay Wenimats. "That is where you'll live. Bring happiness to my people. Whenever my people want you they'll send you these prayer sticks."

Iatiku made one so Tsitsanits would recognize it. For each kind of Katsina she made one, so each would know his own prayer stick. Whenever the prayer sticks were sent the Katsinas would have to respond. After distributing them, Iatiku told Tsitsanits to compose a song which should be pretty so as to give happiness to her people.

This is how Iatiku sent the Katsinas to Wenimats. She told them to wait for prayer sticks and always be prepared to come. "Your people and my people will be combined," she said. "You'll give us food from your world, we'll give you food from ours. Your people are to represent clouds. You're to bring rain and rule the summer clouds."

Iatiku told the Katsinas to take along animals, as they would also be permitted to be hunters. She picked up the basket of corn meal, corn pollen, tobacco, and prayer sticks and opened the road for them four lengths (a long distance) to Wenimats so they could come back when needed. Then she handed Tsitsanits the basket.

Only Kopishtaiya remained. To him she said, "You're to be

separate from the others." He was given the same sort of instructions and prayer sticks and told to go east to where the sun rises. "You'll represent and rule the winter clouds," she said. "My people will pray to you to obtain bravery and long, healthy life. In the winter time they'll send you prayer sticks."

Now she gave him a basket with pollen, corn meal, tobacco, and prayer sticks. She made the road four lengths to the east and back and told his Katsinas to make their home where the sun rises.

This is how Iatiku placed the rulers of the clouds to whom her people would pray.

2 2.

Iatiku builds her people's first houses and village. She teaches them the proper way to invite the Katsinas to visit, using altars and prayer sticks.

When this was done Iatiku thought of leaving. "Now you're going to make homes here," she told her people. When she spoke some sacred words all of a sudden there grew up a house. "This is the kind of house you're going to build to live in," she said. Her people started to build one of their own, using this as a model.

Iatiku gathered some rocks and dirt for them, and then sticks. All of them grew and multiplied until ready for use. So they made a town. Iatiku laid out the plans for the town and the plaza.

Once this was done, she had further instructions. To the first man born to the Antelope clan she said, "You're to be Tiamuni, father of the Katsina here in the pueblo. You're the one to welcome them when they come." Iatiku made him an altar, the first ever created. "Let's try and see if everything works all right," she said. "We'll call the Katsinas."

She showed the people how to make prayer sticks and taught them the prayers. This took four days. She had them bring all their prayer sticks to the Antelope clan altar and place them in baskets until they filled four. Then the entire Antelope clan offered the baskets to the Katsinas and invited them to come. Taking the prayer sticks to the west they buried them. In praying they made four motions so as to cover the four lengths of the road.

Once this was done, the prayer sticks continued on until they reached the Katsinas. There Tsitsanits took them and told each of the Katsinas that they were being called to visit the people at Shipapu (where they still lived). At this the Katsinas prayed to the clouds with the same prayer sticks. Then they smoked the cigarettes that were in the baskets so that the rain clouds would come into them.

Tsitsanits had Messenger Katsina go back to Iatiku's people and alert them that all the Katsinas would arrive on the fourth day. "We're going to bring provisions and corn," he said.

So Messenger Katsina traveled on to tell the people.

23.

This is the first time the people welcome the Katsinas into their community. Arriving in a cloud, the Katsinas sing and dance and pass out presents. Before departing they give people masks and regalia so they can dance on their own.

When Messenger Katsina arrived at Shipapu, Antelope Chief met him to receive his message. When he left Antelope Chief told the people to expect the Katsinas on the fourth day.

Now Iatiku instructed everyone, "Let's also prepare to welcome them with our food." She called for a tribal hunt. Everyone who killed anything prepared it in their own home for the day the Katsinas arrived.

That day they came in a cloud, and everything was brought out for them. In the lead was Messenger Katsina, who announced their approach. They were met by Antelope Chief who pointed out the different places for them to dance on the village plaza—first on the north side, then west, then south, then east. When the Katsinas completed their first round of four dances they were escorted inside, to rest near the altar.

At this time there were still no kivas, the people were just trying this out. But they were interested in the Katsinas and happy over the visit. The Katsinas brought their own songs.

Everyone was instructed to take food to the house where the Katsinas were staying. But they could not enter. Only members of the Antelope clan, who served them, could go in. This was at noon.

In the afternoon, following each dance, the Katsinas gave the people their presents of food. They also handed them throwing-sticks, since bows and arrows did not yet exist.

Before the Katsinas departed, Messenger Katsina announced that they did not wish to leave the people entirely.

They could take the presents and use them for any dance that they wanted to put on, in order to be happy. So before they departed the Katsina stripped, all except for their masks, and gave the people their clothing.

Antelope Chief bade the Katsina goodbye and they left.

24.

To complete the village, Iatiku creates the first kiva,
so in the future the visiting Katsinas will feel at home.
This kiva represents the underworld. She teaches the
people how to behave in this sacred place.

Now Iatiku said, "So far all is well, but some things are
needed yet. We have no kiva. This is the way I emerged, so I
guess we'll make a house in the ground, which we'll call a
kiva. This will be the sacred place for the Katsinas when they
come." At first the kivas were round, now they have corners.
At the foot of the mesa, where the old town was washed
away, the kiva was round.

When they began to build that first kiva, Iatiku told Oak
Man that it should be done in a certain way and showed him
how. The whole kiva was to represent Shipapu, the place of
emergence.

When they built the first kiva, they put up beams of four
different trees. These were the same four trees that were
planted in the underworld for the people to climb on. In the
north, under the foundation, they placed yellow turquoise, in
the west, blue turquoise, in the south, red, and in the east,
white turquoise. Prayer sticks were placed at each location so
the foundation would be strong and never give way. The
walls represented the sky, the beams of the roof (made of
wood of the first four trees) represented the Milky Way. The
sky looks like a circle, hence the round shape of the kiva. The
ladder represented the rainbow.

The medicine man was instructed to make a fireplace inside the kiva. It was put under the ladder and called Bear. In
front of the fireplace was a hollow place in the floor in which
an altar like the one Iatiku first made was kept. It was covered with a board. The medicine men were the only ones allowed to dance on it. It gave out a hollow sound. Iatiku said

that whenever a medicine man wanted more superhuman power he should dance and roll over this altar.

On the north was a hollow, dug-out place that represented the door to North Mountain, East Mountain, West Mountain, Sun, and Moon. Whenever they prayed to these powers, known as the "powers that rule," they prayed into this doorway.

Around the interior of the kiva were the imaginary seats of fog covered with bear skins or lion skins. All this was described in the prayers. The Spirits were invited in prayer to come and sit on these seats. Actually, only fetishes were kept in the kiva. The real Spirits remained out in the mountains of the cardinal points. But they were still invited to come and be present during ceremonies, and that is where they sat.

Iatiku ordered that people should always enter the kiva facing the ladder as soon as they placed a foot upon it. When entering or leaving one should never turn back. This was because when Nautsiti and Iatiku came up from the lower world, they went on up without stopping or turning back. If anyone turned back, it would shorten his life. He would leave his soul in the kiva. If someone did this, his relatives were required to buy back his life by bringing food to the kiva. When they reached the top of the ladder with the food, they would call down to those inside, "Below!"

The ladder, too, should be made of wood from the first four trees of the underworld. Nautsiti and Iatiku did not know where the pine trees touched, nor where a rainbow touches, so they named the ladder "Rainbow."

When one stepped down at the foot of the ladder one should always go to the right and take a seat—never to the left. When one departed, one should circle round to the right. Never take fire from the front of the fireplace. Never step on the fireplace. Never whistle in there.

All these rules Iatiku laid down for proper conduct in the kiva.

25.

For success in the hunt, Iatiku appoints an Eagle
clan man to head a Hunter's Society. Its members
will use the powers of the prey animals against the
game animals. The first proper hunt begins.

"I think someone ought to be the father of the game animals," Iatiku said. "His work will be the power of his songs. When he sings and prays to the animals the hunters will be partners to the prey animals."

Because the eagle is a bird of prey she chose the oldest man born to the Eagle clan. He was to sing with the people when they went to hunt because only he knew the prayers belonging to the prey animals. Iatiku taught him songs and prayers and gave him an altar with which to secure the power of animals that kill.

"Let's try it out and see if it will work," she said. The Eagle Man set up his new altar in his house. Iatiku taught him to make prayer sticks for the men going on a hunt and fetishes representing the beasts of prey. Eagle Man called a meeting at his house for passing on the songs he was taught. All night they sang. This was one of the songs they sang to obtain power from the beasts of prey.

> In the north country,
> The lion, the hunter has come out.
> The sparkling yellow bunch of prayer feathers on its head,
> Tossing, tossing, has gone out.
> I will go bravely to collect spruce and get blessings.
> In the western country,
> The lynx, the hunter has come out.
> The sparkling blue-green bunch of prayer feathers on its head,
> Tossing, tossing, has gone out.
> I will go bravely to collect spruce and get blessings.

In the southern country,
The wild-cat, the hunter has come out.
The sparkling red bunch of prayer feathers on its head,
Tossing, tossing, has gone out.
I will go bravely to collect spruce and get blessings.
In the eastern country,
The wolf, the hunter has come out.
The sparkling white bunch of prayer feathers on its head,
Tossing, tossing, has gone out.
I will go bravely to collect spruce and get blessings.

Early the next morning, Eagle Man gave prayer sticks to each man who sang and told them to go and pray in the wilds. They were now the Hunter's Society and prayed in order to possess the powers of the prey animals.

Early on the fourth morning Eagle Man went out to a place of his choice. On his way whenever he saw animal tracks, even small ones, he picked up some dirt, and also dung, and placed them in a cedar bark container. When he came to the designated place he tied both ends of the cedar bark with yucca blades. Then he started a fire the natural way, with a fire drill. He scorched the dirt and dung so as to burn the feet of the game animals so they could not run fast.

To signal the rest to join him he threw green branches on the fire and made smoke. Eagle Man had already told the men that when they met at the camp they were to bring sacred corn meal and pollen, and gather dung, or dirt from any animals' tracks they passed. When they arrived at his fire they were to throw that in, to help the scorching of their feet.

As they did this they were to speak the name of any prey animal they wished to assist them. Birds for small game like rabbits; lion, wolf, and wildcat for deer and larger game. Upon arriving at camp everyone did this. Usually a high spot was picked as a meeting place, so they could watch and not start hunting if someone was still on their way.

When all had gathered Eagle Man said, "Now we're going north, west, south, or east on a drive, stirring up the game in the brush." Whenever the men halted on their hunt, they should pray with corn meal to Mother Earth so they would not be injured, or be blamed for killing the animals. He chose two men from his clan to lead two lines of men in a wide circle. The lines would meet at a spot which he designated. They were to carry torches of cedar bark fire with them, to signal when this meeting would take place.

26.

The first hunt continues in the proper way—from killing to butchering to skinning to distribution of the meat.

The hunters were to observe several rules. When you threw a stick and hit a game animal, if it did not get up, it was yours. If two sticks hit about the same time and killed the animal, the one who first said "mine" got it. If you hit a rabbit and knocked it down, but it got up and was killed by another, the one who first stopped it got it. Suppose a man started early in the morning tracking an animal, but another started later and came in ahead and killed it. Then it belonged to the one who first started to track it. These rules helped avoid arguments.

After hunting all day they were about to make the final circle. Eagle Man announced that anything killed now belonged to him. On the day after the hunt, those who had killed game were supposed to roast it and ready it for him. Then he would bring it all to Antelope Man. That was why Iatiku made the Antelope Man the leader, so when the Katsinas arrived he could feed them.

Eagle Man made a final announcement about the hunt: "If you get a rabbit, skin it carefully and save the skin. Break the upper part of the legs of the rabbit and fold the front legs across the breast and hind legs across the back." They were to take corn meal and pollen and place them under each leg of the rabbit, then thank Mother Earth and pray that she raise more game. He warned them not to put the rabbit into the fire or coals head first when roasting it. They should face it out so its spirit could escape and be reborn and furnish more game. For its own food the spirit of the rabbit would take the corn and pollen offerings.

When a deer was killed, it should be butchered where it fell. The legs were cut off and the ribs taken out. Head, backbone, and hide were left connected in one piece. When cut open, the entrails were laid on one side. The bladder was removed and placed in the center of the entrails. Then the hunter prayed that the deer be reborn, and that in the future he would have good luck with hunting. Finally he sprinkled corn meal and pollen and pieces of beads and shells on it.

Such were the instructions to the hunters. They were to be followed so they would continue to have game. All of these practices were given by Eagle Man on the first hunt. After this he told the hunters, "You may go home and rest."

27.

Iatiku teaches the making and use of hunting fetishes. Fashioned in the images of beasts of prey, they are owned by families.

When hunters went on a big hunt they got fetishes from Eagle Man to take along. When the hunter took out an animal's heart, the fetish was made to drink its blood. The fetishes were kept in each family. Iatiku made the first one for Eagle Man, then he taught the others.

They should be made of hard stone, flint, or gypsum, with eyes of turquoise set in pitch. Small ones represented the prey animals and were carried for protection. Any man could make a fetish, which he could call wolf, lion, or whatever he pleased. He then brought it to the Eagle Man.

Eagle Man and the Hunter's Society prayed and sang over it. Into it they put the spirit and power of the lion (north), wolf (west), lynx (south), and wildcat (east). The power of the fetish was drawn from all these equally. The head man held the fetish in the palms of his hands and swung it to the four directions to the following song, which was repeated for the wolf, the lynx, and the wildcat.

> It comes alive
> It comes alive, alive, alive.
> In the north mountain
> The lion comes alive
> In the north mountain, comes alive.
> With this the prey animal
> Will have power to attract deer, antelope;
> Will have power to be lucky.

With each verse the Eagle Man faced the direction indicated and swung his hands. He prayed one way and did not join in with the other singers. In the kiva was one large fetish which represented each of the four beasts of prey—lion, wolf, lynx, and wildcat. Whenever the song was over a fetish was laid in front of the altar. The one to be given life was placed beside the fetish for which it was named. This was its "mother," from which it drew its power. Thereafter it lived as her offspring. Each society member approached the fetish in turn and said, "Drink the blood of the lion (or whatever prey animal it has been named)." There it remained overnight and came alive.

The next day it was returned to its owner. But it still had a tie with the one on the altar. It could be recalled from the owner if the society wanted to use it. Often this was done when an owner was especially lucky in the hunt. When the society finished with it, it went back to him. These fetishes were handed down within the family.

28.

Iatiku teaches the people how to respect dead animals so they will be reborn. She explains how they should welcome the carcasses, eat their flesh, and care for their skulls.

After a hunter killed an antelope or a deer he packed it into the pueblo. The father or mother in the hunter's house came out with a handful of corn meal and made a "road" into the house and up the ladder—if they lived on an upper story. Then they helped the hunter and laid the deer on the floor with its head towards the fireplace, about ten feet from the fire. Beads were placed on the neck for the deer to wear back to where its spirit was going. In about an hour, when the people thought that its spirit had left, they were removed.

If relatives of the hunter entered, they went up to the deer and touched it and rubbed their hands over their faces. This was because, they said, the deer was pretty and not lazy. To the deer they said, "We're glad you have come to our home and are not ashamed of our people."

A dish of corn meal was placed nearby, every visitor fed a little to the deer. They asked him to come to their house next, for they believed it would be reborn. When the beads were taken off, they blew them into the other room.

Then they started skinning the animal up to the neck. The entire hide was taken off. The head was boiled in a pot without taking off the horns. In the pot were added corn, pumpkin seeds, and piñon nuts. These were called the deer's earrings.

Before they ate this, the hunter called for his father's clan to come and eat the head. If she was living, the mother of the hunter's father took the eyes and ate them. If she was not alive, the oldest female relative in the father's clan did so. The hunter, or any man, was not supposed to eat the eyes lest he always have tears and be unable to see far. Nor should the hunter eat the tongue as this would make him thirsty. Nor may he eat the soft udder or his teeth would not be strong.

After the meat was eaten from the head, the skull was placed on top of the house to dry. When he had time, the hunter took it back into the mountains where he prayed that the deer would come alive again. First it should be painted as the deer was originally. A black line was drawn down the middle of the face. Under the jaw was painted white. Balls of cotton were stuffed in the eye sockets with the centers painted black. A string was tied across the antlers with feathers attached to it.

All large game was treated like this—mountain sheep, elk, and buffalo; also lions, lynx, and bear. Rabbit skulls were treated similarly, except that they were not painted or prepared in any way.

This is how Iatiku made the first Hunter's Society.

29.

The Katsinas are invited for a second visit. Iatiku creates the office of War Chief to help the Antelope clan greet them and keep the people together.

All the game was gathered and saved for the Katsinas at the house of the Antelope clan. After this the men who had been taught the hunting songs composed songs of their own to rejoice over the hunt. They put on a dance in honor of Eagle Man and proclaimed him leader of the hunt.

"Let's try to call the Katsinas again," Iatiku said. So she asked Antelope Man to do this. He notified the people to pray for another Katsina visit, and to bring their prayer sticks to his altar. Antelope Man took baskets full of them and prayed and buried them. Then the prayer sticks were received at Wenimats—where the Katsinas lived under the lake.

So it happened as before. Again the Messenger Katsina was sent to alert the people that the Katsinas would arrive on the fourth day. Four women from the Antelope clan were selected to prepare the food that was brought in by Eagle Man for the feast. Every household was asked to contribute maize flour to the Antelope clan altar. The four women prepared this for the Katsinas.

The earlier time, Iatiku had the people bring food to the door where the Katsinas were staying. That visit was informal. Then the Katsinas were treated much as human visitors. This time she had called for the community hunt, so the people would not have to come around again. Now only members of the Antelope clan were permitted to serve the Katsinas.

Everything happened properly. The Katsinas were taken care of at the Antelope clan altar. "All's well," Iatiku said. "Now it doesn't seem to me that we're playing with the Katsinas. Now they're to be regarded as sacred." Everything worked well, but

Iatiku saw that the Antelope clan was carrying too much of the burden.

So she thought of making another officer who would be called War Chief. For this office she chose the first man in the Sky clan, because he was to rule on the outside. He would rank above Eagle Man and the other officers. Whatever he said went. In the old days this position always went to the Sky clan.

Iatiku called this man and said, "I'm going to make you War Chief." For him she prepared what is called a "Broken Prayer Stick." It had the four trails marked on the four sides. They extended from the earth up to the sky. As she gave it to him she said, "When you clasp this in your hands, you're drawing the people together so they won't be scattered. With this you'll have power over all the rest of them. You'll have them tucked under your arms, and their minds will be tucked in your temples." By this she meant, "You'll do their thinking for them and speak for them. You'll be their mind."

Iatiku taught him the prayers. They should always start from Shipapu. After coming up from Shipapu, the prayers were to start from the north and take in the west, south, and east. It was a very long prayer.

This War Chief was told that he would rule around these places but was not paid for his services. He would represent the people and pray for them.

30.

Iatiku creates the office of Country Chief. With his two helpers he will notify everyone of the comings and goings of the Katsinas, pray to the sacred directions, track the seasons, oversee the gardens, and determine the solstices.

Before this the Antelope clan ruled everything. Now Iatiku created Country Chief and told him that he would have the hardest duty. He would be the one to go out and meet the Katsinas and bring their message to the Antelope clan. He would also notify the people by crying out matters of importance relating to the outside.

Iatiku said, "Let's try to call the Katsinas." At this time they remained at Shipapu. All was done as before, only now Iatiku said things worked out better. However, she saw that Country Chief was carrying too much of the load and thought of giving him helpers.

She selected the first two sons (or maybe brothers) of Country Chief. She called the oldest one, who would be next in rank, Wren Youth. The other was Mocking Bird Youth. Iatiku named them so because they were to represent these birds and make their sounds and bring messages to the people, thus relieving Country Chief. It is different now. Today they call them the two cooks because they serve the head man. They prepare his corn meal and pollen so he will always have plenty. Now they have Spanish names.

Every fourth day Country Chief went out to pray to the north, after another four days to the west, another four days to the south, and four more days to the east. (Today they take turns, and the three of them do it, making the burden easier. These helpers also assist as town criers.)

Everything was tried out again, and Iatiku was satisfied.

Country Chief was also told to watch the seasons. Each

day he was expected to go out in the country and observe the plants. At this time the only way they could tell the seasons was by their growth. Country Chief was supposed to tell everyone what season was ending or approaching. It is told in later tradition that Country Chief started to watch the stars and moon. Being able to tell seasons more accurately this way, he abandoned the method of watching the plants. Country Chief also watched the sun to determine the time for solstices. Now the Antelope Chief does this.

The Katsinas that live in the east were to come for the winter solstice, and those that live in the west for the summer solstice.

31.

After a while prayer sticks are made to invite the Katsinas of the east, who are called Kopishtaiya. Their visit is successful. These Katsinas pray, offer spiritual protection, and distribute seeds.

For a long time the people lived with these officers.

When everything seemed all right with the Katsinas of the west, Iatiku decided to try the Katsinas of the east, who are called Kopishtaiya. So she had Country Chief inform Antelope Man that they were going to try and call the Kopishtaiya who live where the sun comes up, and to make ready. "It's all right," Antelope Man said. "Tell the people to wait for them and prepare by gathering material to make prayer sticks."

Country Chief instructed his two helpers how to do this. Before cutting sticks for prayer sticks they should pray: "Come and help us, Yellow Flint! Come, Red Flint! Come, White Flint! Help us! You're the ones who're really going to cut the prayer sticks."

He taught them what to sing when they used the flints to cut the prayer sticks. Greeting his helpers, Country Chief made a trail for them to come inside as they brought their sticks. When they stopped outside they called out, "Inside," so as not to interrupt any ceremony that might be under way. Nowadays they knock on the door.

On the fourth day all the prayer sticks were brought in. They resembled the ones originally given to the Kopishtaiya by Iatiku. Antelope Man walked to the east, carrying them in baskets, and prayed and buried them. Four days later, he said, the people should expect the Kopishtaiya. Although they had no Messenger figure like the Katsinas of the west, the people were sure they would show.

Just before sun-up Country Chief heard them singing in the east and sent messages to the village that the Kopishtaiya were near. They were naked save for breech cloths made of rabbit skins. Even though it was cold, they wore no moccasins, for they represented strong, hardy men. The Kopishtaiya were not dancers, they only circled the village. At intervals they went around and prayed and put up spiritual protections.

The people saw their bags of seeds. These they presented to everyone and told them to plant. They thanked the people for praying with prayer sticks and food, and then they left.

Iatiku saw that they were real and that all went well. So she told the people to believe in them also.

32.

A plague prompts Iatiku to have the officials select a man from the Oak clan to be the first curer, or medicine man. She directs him to North Mountain to collect obsidian, pieces from a tree struck by lightning, and the arrowhead that hit the tree.

Some time after this the evil spirit, the snake, came to Iatiku's people in the form of disease. By this time it had grown of itself into a big power, and the people came down with plague. It is not known what form of disease it was, for they had not experienced sickness before.

The people were panic stricken. They tried to relieve themselves in every way, gathering plants and making drinks. Nothing helped. So Iatiku thought of choosing a man to be known as a Medicine Man. She told Country Chief what she was thinking and he agreed. Then Iatiku said, "I've told you to watch your people and to know them, so I'll leave it up to you to choose the man." She wanted Antelope Man and Eagle Man to join a council with the three Country Chiefs.

So far no one had died. At the meeting Country Chief stood up and said that he was selecting the first and oldest from the Oak clan as the first Medicine Man. His altar would be named "fire medicine man." He represented strong wood for making fire, and his altar used fire, one of Iatiku's first strong gifts. All agreed so Country Chief told Iatiku the altar's name and said, "This is the one we have chosen." When the Oak clan man was notified to come to the broken prayer stick he learned that he had been chosen to help whenever sickness came. "You'll be the means of their recovery," they told him.

Iatiku instructed and cared for him and gave him his healing altar and paraphernalia. First she had him go to North Mountain and look for a pine tree that was struck by lightning. He was to take some split wood from the blasted part. "You'll also find obsidian which will also be used by you," she added.

She showed him how to make the black prayer stick as a symbol of darkness, for he was to work at night. He was to make four and carry them when he went looking for the pine and obsidian. "You'll also find an arrowhead with which the pine was struck down," she said. Even today at Acoma they think an arrowhead is left wherever lightning has struck. These are sought and worn as amulets.

With this arrowhead he would have protection. It would be his heart or soul.

33.

*The Oak clan man learns to be a medicine man.
He acquires an altar and songs, and bear and eagle
helpers. Pottery is created so he can mix his medicine in a painted bowl.*

Taking the four prayer sticks to the north, Oak Man prayed
with them before burying them. He searched for the pine
tree and found everything as Iatiku had said. He gathered
the flat split wood into a bundle, picked up some obsidian
and the arrowhead, and brought them back.

His relatives and clan knew why he was gone and were
waiting. When Oak Man told Iatiku that he had fulfilled
her instructions she said that he should make an altar for
himself, using the obsidian for a knife. She taught him how
to make it, and to make common prayer sticks. That altar is
usually known by her name.

Next Iatiku had Oak Man make a sand painting. It is
blue and circular and represents the sky. The earth hangs
from the Milky Way, because the Milky Way is like a roof
beam holding up the earth and because the Milky Way does
not change position but is always circling in the east. The
head of the earth faces east. The feet are in the west, with
arms outstretched north and south. As the earth lies facing
upward, the sun rises over its head and passes over its body
lengthwise, setting at its feet. This was what they sang when
they made that first altar of the earth.

> Earth plant, earth plant,
> Your arm is stretched towards the north,
> Your legs are stretched towards the west,
> Another arm is stretched towards the south,
> Your head is stretched towards the east.
> You are centered in the middle.

From the center all plants grow up.
At the center you are inhabited with people.
From the center outward, all breath is breathed.
The earth lies spread out like a plant.

With a special prayer the medicine bowl was placed on the heart of the earth. Thus the medicine drew its strength from there. The Sun, Moon, and Stars were drawn as alive, with eyes and mouth. Sun, Moon, and Stars are the most powerful of forces. Sun gives everything strength. It gives the seeds in the earth the strength to sprout. This strength is imparted to us when we eat these plants.

Iatiku taught Oak Man the songs and showed him how to make two fetishes to represent bears. He would possess their powers. To the bear fetish she said, "You'll be a partner to this medicine man." She told the eagle he would also be his partner. The bear represented the power of all animals that live on earth, the eagle of all birds that fly in the air. Iatiku had the weasel be a partner as well and represent the animals that live in the ground.

Next Iatiku had Oak Man's wife make a square medicine bowl from fine clay. After she fashioned it Iatiku told her to draw two bears on the front, an eagle on the back, and the weasel on the bottom. This was the origin of pottery.

34.

The instructions continue. Iatiku teaches the medicine man to use bear and weasel paws, eagle feathers, and blood from all three, together with shells and stone beads to form his altar. Lastly they make a drum and a rattle.

This bowl was for mixing medicine. Iatiku had Oak Man gather spruce and fir branches, a sweet root, and one other root and grind them together. He was also to obtain the left front paw of a bear and skin it a little above the wrist with the claws still on. "Get the left front paw because that's the bear's best hand," she said. "Bears are quicker on the left." From claws of the other three feet he was to make a necklace, then place the bearskin behind the altar. The two bear fetishes were to be painted with the bear's blood.

On the altar were also two eagle and two weasel fetishes. Oak Man was to kill an eagle and take the longest feather from each wing, the down from under the tail, and tie them on the top of the altar's two uprights. Iatiku had him kill a weasel, place the skin as the altar's foundation, and add its two front paws to the fetish. They look like human hands, and that is how a weasel uses them. Blood from an eagle's heart was used to paint the eagle fetishes, while weasel blood was smeared on the weasel fetishes.

Iatiku told Oak Man to kill a mallard duck, skin it, and bring the green wing feathers to the altar. From an abalone shell, and from turquoise from the mountain of the west, he was to make a string of beads. Iatiku said this would be something sacred, and taught him how to grind the beads. But he was not to throw the broken chips away. She said, "These chips are also sacred and you'll use them to pray with."

One thing remained. "You're to make a drum and a rattle," she said. "The drum will come from a certain tree that grows a layer each year. Knock the center out and use the outside cylinder. Cover both ends with elk hide." She showed him how to lace it on. Then she had him make the drumstick out of the same tree.

When the drum was finished he was to make the rattle. "Take the scrotum of the elk," she said. "Scrape off the hair and stuff it with dry sand. Let it dry and tie a stick in it first. When it's dry, pour the sand out. Then put some agave seeds into it." Thus it was finished.

35.

With Oak Man's help, Iatiku creates a Honani, the fetish made from a perfectly kerneled ear of corn. It represents herself and she breathes life into it. Oak Man learns the songs and prayers for his altar and prepares to try it out.

At this time Iatiku lived alone in a house on an island in a lake. She lived here and the people lived all around her. But only Country Chief visited her. While getting his instructions for making the altar, he ran back and forth to the island. Then Country Chief passed them on to Oak Man.

Iatiku announced, "Now it's my turn. I'll make you a Honani." She told Oak Man to bring her the eagle and duck feathers that were not used on the altar. She added a road-runner's tail feathers, a magpie's tail feathers, cotton, and an ear of corn with kernels clear up and no open space at the top of the cob. They are very rare.

With these things in hand she told Country Chief and his helpers to guard her house. She wanted the place to be secret and no one bothering her. The trail to her house was paved with abalone shell which came from this lake.

Iatiku made her fetish with the ear of corn in the center. Into the hollow in the bottom of the cob she blew her breath. This meant her own power, for she had blown her heart, or soul, into it. She added some honey into the hollow as food for her breath. Honey comes from all kinds of plants and stands for all plant foods. Putting it in the cob also meant that it would be the seed or source for all food to come. Then she stoppered the cob with cotton and wrapped it in four layers of corn husk.

Now Iatiku took the skin of the duck's head and a turquoise and laid them under the corn, as its seat. Over the top and around the outside husks she spread cotton. The duck skin with blue feathers was placed under the turquoise because the color was similar. From now on the turquoise was going to have a lot of power, the power to make one attractive and be loved.

The breath that Iatiku blew into the cob would be powerful as far as the air extended, but no farther. She used roadrunner, magpie, eagle down, and turkey feathers (the short tail feathers—there were no parrots yet), and the down from under the eagle's tail. From then on these feathers were to be useful in making prayers. The green wing feathers of the duck were put in front to hide the face. Finally a string of abalone, turquoise, and shell beads were placed above the fetish.

All that went into the making of the fetish was to be regarded as sacred. The whole thing represented Iatiku. She planned to leave it behind, as she was thinking of leaving her people.

Oak Man was present throughout this process so that when necessary he could make another. When a man becomes a medicine man is the only time one of these fetishes is made. After Iatiku taught Oak Man all this she showed him how to make another altar. It took a long time to learn its prayers and songs.

"Let's try it out," she said. "You must work four days, and for these days you must not touch a woman. You will eat special food during this time: beans without salt, corn (and other plants). None of this can be mixed with meat." The fourth night he would try out the altar.

36.

Iatiku's magical basket produces Koshari, the first sacred clown. He acts crazy, talks loudly, bumps into officials, and amuses Oak Man, his new partner.

In Iatiku's basket were three more things. She knew there were the two eggs, one parrot and one crow, but the third thing she did not know. She decided to bring it to life and see what it was. "Come alive!" she said. "Let's see what you're like." At her words it began to speak. "Why have I come alive," it asked, "am I wanted?" Iatiku replied, "Don't ask. You'll be useful."

It came to life in the form of a male human. Koshari was kind of crazy, always active, picking around, talking nonsense, speaking backwards, and so forth. Iatiku did not think much of him, so she sent him to Oak Man to see if he could be of any use there. But first she said, "I'm going to initiate you. I'm going to be there myself."

So Koshari went to Oak Man, saying, "I know everything. Sure I'll go and I'll do everything for him. I'll be a big help." He said this even though he was just born and had no experience at all.

Rushing to the pueblo, Koshari climbed the wall to get in, and began asking everyone where Oak Man's altar was. He spoke loudly around the altar, even though it is supposed to be quiet there. When he finally bumped into Country Chief, who was guarding the place, Koshari demanded, "Where's the kiva of the medicine man?"

When he tried to rush in Country Chief caught him. "But I've been sent here," Koshari protested. "I'm allowed everywhere by Iatiku." So Country Chief let him go, saying, "Well, he may be of some use."

Koshari yelled into the kiva, "I'm coming down." Without awaiting response or permission, he descended. Reaching the floor he said, "I've come as your partner. I've been sent to help you. I can do anything."

Oak Man was glad for the help, but Koshari was impatient. He went right to work and placed the different objects in front of the altar, insisting, "Let me do it. I can do it." Nor did Oak Man prevent him. With his garbled speech and wisecracking and self-confidence, Koshari brought amusement into Oak Man's solitary life.

37.

Before Oak Man ends his fast, he and Koshari
sing over Iatiku's altar and her fetish. After the
people present food before the altar and the fetish,
Iatiku returns it to them to eat.

On the fourth day of Oak Man's preparatory fast Iatiku had him build a fire in front of the altar and ready some yellow corn. She also told Country Chief to have the people wait quietly for four days, as she would bring the fetish to life. Country Chief told everyone that Oak Man, the medicine man, was fasting for four days. On the fourth day they should cook for him.

Once it grew dark, Koshari spoke up. "It's time, let me go after Iatiku." He went and got her. Coming to the kiva roof, she called down, "Chima!" Having rushed down ahead of her, Koshari answered back, "Come on in, it's all right with us." Entering the kiva Iatiku said, "Greetings, mother, and my officers. From now on it will be by you that the pueblo will be run." Both Koshari and Oak Man responded, "All right, but it comes from you."

Taking her by the hand, Koshari set Iatiku down behind her altar. She asked Oak Man if Koshari had been of any use. "Yes, he's been very helpful," Oak Man replied. "Yes, I know," Koshari added, "I'm an expert at all this."

Oak Man wanted to know if everything was all right, if the altar suitably represented her. "Yes, I'll give myself to be represented by this altar and fetish," she answered. "It will represent long life, luck, harvest, and game. The altar will have power over all of these." And she asked Oak Man to pass "my sister" (the fetish) to her.

They started to sing the song that was to establish the altar and give it life—so it could represent Iatiku. Here is that song, which is sung four times.

Iatiku's ear of corn fetish is set up.
Iatiku's ear of corn fetish is set up.
For the sake of the common people
Iatiku's ear of corn fetish is set up, is set up.
Iatiku's ear of corn fetish is set up.
For the sake of the earth
Iatiku's ear of corn fetish is set up.
Iatiku, sit down here,
Sit down here, sit down here.

Singing the loudest, Koshari stayed a verse or so ahead of the rest. Once that was over, Iatiku had Oak Man tell the people that wished to bring food for the altar and the medicine man to enter. Immediately Koshari stood up. "Let me climb up and tell this to Country Chief," he said. "I'm ready to eat," he proclaimed, "bring the food." The families that had been selected by Country Chief came down.

By now it was dark. Iatiku told Oak Man to offer the food to "the ones that are ahead of you," which meant the now-living altar. Gesturing the food towards the altar and the spirits, Oak Man prayed. "I'm just a common man," he said. "I'm not superhuman. My hands have no skill." All the while Koshari was imitating everything he was doing.

Iatiku had Oak Man partake of some food. "When you finish," she said, "you must offer it to the earth the next day, thus giving it back." And she added, "Now that you've set this offering aside, you may break your fast on what is left over."

No sooner had she said this than Koshari started to eat.

38.

Everyone is welcomed to Iatiku's altar. During the night she shows Oak Man and Koshari how to make the first healing medicine. With it Oak Man extracts sickness from the people.

After they broke fast, Koshari was sent out with a message that all the people were to enter. Everyone, it will be remembered, was sick. They came to wish Oak Man luck.

Now Iatiku began to initiate Oak Man in the use of her altar, and also Koshari. During their first song Iatiku had Oak Man take corn and stir it into the hot coals with his bare hands. Koshari did this, too. After the corn was parched, Oak Man jumped into the hot coals and threw them over his chest and body. Now he became a full member of the altar and it belonged to him.

Other songs followed. "The next thing you're going to do is make medicine," said Iatiku. First they collected water— yellow water of the north, blue water of the west, red water of the south, white water of the east. The water is not actually colored, this is just in the song. For each direction the names of the mountains were called. After they finished the water song, they poured the water, one shell-full at a time, as each direction was named. Then the song for getting herbs for the medicine was sung. Some of the medicine was taken and then came another song—a prayer for powers to come to the medicine from the north, the east, the south, and the west.

At one time during the medicine-making they smoked. Iatiku told Oak Man to roll a cigarette and put honey on the end that goes into the mouth. This made the tobacco more powerful, enabling it to reach out and be appreciated. Thus when the medicine man smokes this sacred tobacco mixed with the honey that represents all food, the smoke goes into the air and is carried by the air to all the people, entering them and healing and nourishing them. They had known about tobacco for a long time, but they had not known about adding honey.

After the medicine was mixed, another song gave it to the altar. Eagle feathers were dipped in it and sprinkled over the altar and then Oak Man sprinkled it over the audience. Bringing some ashes and placing them before the altar, Koshari did the same, dipping the tips of the feathers under them and sprinkling the people. This lasted all night.

Iatiku had Oak Man put on the bear paw like a glove. The fetish he took with his right hand, the arrowhead in his left. The people were naked and sitting on the ground. Iatiku told Oak Man to dampen his eyes with the medicine. This opened them so he could see into every one of them. To each, in turn, he touched on the head, the shoulders, knees, and feet, while the singing and praying went on. Each time a person was touched he or she inhaled deeply and the medicine man blew the spirit of Iatiku towards them.

Now Oak Man went among the people and sucked the sickness from each of their chests (over the heart). He spit it into his palm and cast it out. When he was done sucking he gave everyone a drink of a shell containing medicine, just a mouthful.

Then Koshari also administered this medicine.

39.

Iatiku establishes four societies of medicine men, together with their initiation rituals. From now on Country Chief will tell them when to cure and will arrange their initiations. Iatiku has Koshari live with the Sun to be his helper.

Their work took until daybreak. Only then were the people told they could leave, and a dismissal song was sung. Before they left Oak Man stood up to explain that Iatiku had said that the altar was to represent her. "We'll call it our mother. She gives it to us forever, and the medicine men will have it for healing sickness." Then everyone was told to rest.

But Iatiku remained and said to Oak Man, "Now you know everything. But I can see you need helpers. You must make other groups of medicine men." She said they were to be named Flint, Spider, and Giant. These four—Fire, Flint, Spider, and Giant—are the only ones in the tradition. As for the Fire medicine men, she instructed Oak Man to make altars for them similar to his.

To recruit these three other medicine men, Iatiku said, "If any should be sick and wish for long life and come and say they wish to become medicine men, initiate the first man or woman to say this and give them their first altar. To the second give the second altar. To the third, the third altar."

She went on, "There's another way to take people into your order. During the four days of fasting, if anyone enters your place you're to take him as your child and initiate him. And there's still another way to initiate. It's through tobacco. If anyone should roll a cigarette in the corner and give it to you without lighting it, you're to take this person and initiate him."

The people learned all this and found that this ceremony had cured them. Oak Man was told to dismantle the altar carefully and pack it away. "Leave all this in a room other than the kiva," Iatiku said. "But take the fetish home where you may watch it and love it and never forget to feed it before you eat yourself.

"Now you must rest," she said. "Any time Country Chief wants you to cure his people he'll tell you and you must obey him. If anyone comes to you wanting to be a member of your order, tell Country Chief and he'll help arrange it."

To Koshari she said, "You've done your work faithfully. But you're not acting normally enough to remain here with the people." The Koshari was different from the other people because he knew something about himself.

Iatiku wanted him to go and live at the house of the Sun. "You'll help the Sun. At times you may also be called to help here. You'll never be afraid of anything or regard anything as sacred. You'll be allowed everywhere."

She painted him white with black stripes around his body. "This is to be your outfit," she said. Iatiku took some things from the altar and gave them to Koshari, saying, "You'll use those." He thanked her, but said, "I can make more to it and get what I want." So Koshari went and lives today with the Sun, whom he helps.

40.

Iatiku creates another medicine man to represent her husband. Within the kiva he forms a fetish of himself and composes his own songs and sand painting and altar to accompany hers.

It happened that a man came and wanted to be a medicine man. So Oak Man said he would be a Kapina medicine man. When Oak Man asked Iatiku what this medicine man would represent, she answered that would be her husband, Tiamuni. She said he would tell how his altar should be made.

This man told Oak Man to gather two ears of corn, one long one to represent the male, another short one to represent the female. The materials needed were the same as for Iatiku's fetish, except that more feathers were necessary. He was to gather them from as many birds of prey as possible.

After this was done the man showed Oak Man how to finish the fetish. He blew into the corn ear, but in his breath he added flesh from the kangaroo mouse. Since this was the first animal which the sisters were given to eat, it stood for all animal food. This ensured the people of always having meat. If a man wanted to go on a hunt, he must first go to this altar, for it represented all food animals. Since he was a male, Tiamuni's breath also represented bravery, initiative, strength, and long life. Then the cob was closed up with cotton, covered halfway up with buckskin, and its "seat" was abalone shell wrapped in cotton.

Tiamuni also taught Oak Man how to make the earth drawing for this altar. It was like the other female fetish altar, representing the "mother" of the people. Only the tracks of different game animals were on the center of the earth figure. It was gray, but then the directional colors for north, south, east, and west were added. His songs were different from those sung before Iatiku's altar. Nor was this altar to cure the sick, like hers. This one would give strength to the people. Its foundation was of "sky stone" to represent the sky.

Altars in the kiva were always set on the north side, in the direction of Shipapu, the emergence place. Facing south, on the altar's right side stood the larger, male fetish, on the left the smaller female. They were more than a foot thick, and as high as a man or woman. The female was like a mother "guardian angel" who represented the instincts of maternity towards the people and held them in her affection and her heart. The male represented power and virility.

4 1.

This new altar is not for curing but to give the people strength. Initiates into this new Kapina Society are brought before it. Food is offered to the two fetishes. As the initiates are struck with yucca blades soaked in medicine, their investiture is complete. Then comes the people's turn to offer feathers and receive power from the yucca blades.

When all was ready, Country Chief went for Iatiku's husband. The one to be initiated took him by the hand and sat him behind the altar. The ceremony's first song gave life to the altar's medicine bowl. Another song was about the trees of the differently colored directions. With his feathers the medicine man sprinkled water on the fetishes, bringing them to life. Out came the man and woman to be initiated.

Taking the medicine in a shell, he gave some to each. Then they passed large yucca blades to Iatiku's husband. "Here's my life," Country Chief told the initiate. "With these blades you will clothe yourself with manliness and athleticism." So he handed the blades to him. "Here's my mother," he said. "You'll keep our life stored here and our nourishment will be from you." And he handed a basket to the female initiate.

When they finished it was time to feed the fetishes. So Country Chief informed the people, who brought food to the door and offered it to the spirits of the different directions. When they left, the initiates ate. Then the people returned.

Now came the initiation proper. Standing before the altar, Iatiku's husband dipped the yucca blades in the mixed medicine. The two were brought to the hollow place in the kiva, holding the basket between them. From behind the altar Oak Man began singing and the two danced in place. At the part of the song called "fog," Iatiku's husband struck the male four times on the back with the blades. Then the man held the basket while the woman was struck. This completed the initiation.

Those who had brought feather offerings to the two fetishes were told it was their turn. All walked to the front, carrying their feathers and praying. Two medicine people received their feathers, the male medicine man person putting them on the male fetish, the female on the female.

Another song was sung. Those who brought feathers lined up. Iatiku's husband gave the yucca blades to the new medicine man, saying that he now knew how to impart their powers. Country Chief walked past, followed by his two helpers, each in turn holding the basket together with the female medicine person. Each was struck four times on the back.

So ended the ceremony. The people returned home with instructions that the altar must be properly cared for. They were reminded that now they knew the work it was intended to do, which still did not have to do with curing sickness.

42.

A flood brings a second wave of illness. To face this threat yet another medicine man's society is created. The powers of this Flint Society are fire, clouds, and lightning.

For a long time all was well. These two societies of medicine men served the people. But then came more sickness, which they could not cure. So Oak Man thought of making another order, the Flint Society, to help him.

Again it was up to Oak Man to initiate the rest of the medicine societies, but Iatiku still wanted to provide their names. Flint medicine men were to heal any sickness brought by clouds and lightning. It was called Flint because that was the projectile left from lightning which strikes from the clouds.

Three initiates came to Oak Man to be given the Flint altar, which was exactly like the Fire altar. Only the name would be Flint and the songs would be different.

The initiation was also the same as before—getting sticks and so forth from where lightning had struck, the four-day fast, and the meetings they would have. Each initiate was also given prayer sticks through the same rites as with the Fire Society. Their fetishes were given life by singing as before, and there was the initiation with hot coals.

A big flood brought the sickness. The altar's medicine was mixed the same way, but it was made out of the "heart" of concretions that were formed when the wind rolled balls of clay down the arroyos. The centers are removed and ground up with a certain root which braids as it grows and represents the lightning.

The initiates were taught how to paint clouds on kiva walls and acquire power from these images by rubbing their backs against them—the north wall first. Added to the altar was a stick made from lightning-blasted pine or spruce. During their induction Oak Man struck the initiates on the heart and back with it, giving them its power.

On his left hand the Flint Society medicine man wore a longer bear paw, reaching to his elbow. One of the three initiates was put in charge of the altar, but each looked after their own fetish.

Everything went as before. The people brought food to break their four-day fast and were cured of sickness. This Flint Society helped the Fire Society by strengthening it with its powers of lightning and the clouds.

43·

Iatiku teaches the Fire Society medicine men how to bless newborn babies by offering them to the Sun. Lastly she forms the Giant medicine society. Together with the Fire, Kapina, and Flint societies, now there are four.

When Fire Altar Man was learning his duties from Iatiku she told him that he would also have the power to present a child to the Sun four days after its birth, and to name it. This right was handed down to each successive medicine man.

First the child's father went to a medicine man bearing corn meal. With a prayer he requested that he offer the child to the Sun. On the fourth day, at about three in the morning, the medicine man carried his special prayer stick to the baby's house. On the north side of the room he made a sand painting like the one on his altar. On its "heart" he laid the prayer stick. As he set this up he sang prayers and mixed medicine for the child and family.

When the sun was about to rise he took the child outdoors and held it where the sun would shine on it first. As the sun appeared he prayed and gave the baby its personal name and clan name. In his prayers he asked that the baby might have a long healthy life.

Then he motioned four times, from the sun towards the child. Each time this brought the sun's strength into the child. "Now you've become a member of (such and such) clan," he said. The medicine man turned to his left, as when leaving a kiva, and carried the child back to its home.

Upon arriving there the medicine man called out, "Here comes . . ." And he used whatever name the baby had been given. The parents replied, "Oh, yes, let him come in." The medicine man went on, "He's coming in. He's bringing food, beads, game, and a long life into his house."

Once he stepped inside the mother took back her child. With four gestures she waved inside all the food, pots, beads, game, etc., that the child was bringing (figuratively) into the house. The parents had readied food for the altar and the medicine man. All entered and ate. Following this the medicine man made a departing speech and prayer and was handed food to take home.

Next to be formed was the Giant Society. Now this made four societies: Fire, Kapina, Flint, and Giant. Also at Acoma were the Ant and Eagle societies, but they are not covered by the tradition.

44.

All is well, but Iatiku feels the people need more joy. When she encourages them to hold public dances, the leaders send a prayer stick invitation to Koshari. He returns and shows them how to have fun.

Iatiku was pleased with her people, and how the various officials and medicine men were functioning. A long time passed. Then she noticed that everyone was behaving in such a solemn and secret way. She thought they should have something public that everyone could enjoy without the fasting.

Remembering the attire and regalia that the Katsina had presented to the people, she called Country Chief to a council. "Why not call the people to a dance of thanksgiving for the crops and game they've enjoyed," she said. Pleased by the idea, Country Chief had the people meet in the kiva.

He told everyone to compose their own songs. The dance would include everyone who wanted to join—boys, girls, men, and women. Since the Katsinas danced with just one foot, and that was the only dancing they had ever seen, the people suggested they move like them. But when Iatiku instructed the people about the Katsinas, she emphasized that they were sacred and not to be imitated in any way. This new dance was not sacred, so Country Chief reminded them, "No! This is your dance. You must do it in a different way."

They spent four days preparing and making up songs and rehearsing. Everyone was happy and full of anticipation. The whole pueblo was stirred up. Country Chief kept suggesting they call upon Koshari. Since he did not know any new ways to dance, he hoped Koshari could arrange the dancing and teach it to the people. That was his power.

Country Chief said to his two helpers, "I'll try out Koshari and see if he'll come. He talks a lot and seems to know everything." He made a prayer stick and prayed and rolled a cigarette for him. The prayer stick reached Koshari. On the morning of the fourth day he arrived, still painted in stripes, his hair still in a topknot on his head. He asked for Country Chief. "Am I needed here? Have I been called to this place?"

He was taken to the kiva and Country Chief. "Yes, I want you here," Country Chief said. "Now I believe that you're real and have power. My people are going to have a dance and you can arrange it as you wish." He explained its purpose. But even before he finished Koshari knew all about it. "Yes, I'll arrange it for you," he said. Country Chief told everyone to obey Koshari.

First he went from house to house telling people to hurry and come out. They were very interested in Koshari and obeyed. "All who want to dance come to the kiva," Koshari said. He would show them how to paint themselves and don their regalia. As he went through the pueblo Koshari spied the drum belonging to the medicine man. Even though it was only for sacred purposes, without asking permission he grabbed it. He also seized a medicine man's rattle, saying only, "This is needed."

Preparing to rehearse in the kiva, he chose two dance leaders. To one he gave the rattle. To the other, the singer, he handed the drum. All the men lined up. Behind each one he placed a woman, and behind each boy, a girl. Standing in front of them he lifted one foot after another and told the men, "This is how you'll dance." He showed the women how to wave their arms in time with the drum. "You'll dance this way," he said.

The spectators anxiously waited outside. Koshari had the drummer leave the kiva first and beat his drum while everyone watched. Out came the singers, followed by the dancers. Koshari lined them up in the order they were to proceed to the plaza. This was the first song he had them sing.

Yes, my old friends.
Let's go east, to the eastern lake.
It was by the Sun's power, my father,
That I have returned here.

It was by the Moon's power, my father,
That I have returned.
Yes, my old friends.
Let's go east, to the eastern lake.
It was by the Sun's power, my father,
That I have returned.

Everyone was joyful because Koshari was making fun all the while. He was talking backwards, everything he said meant the opposite. The ones who were about to sing he called "grapes" because he had bunched them together.

All morning the dancing went on, until Koshari dismissed them at noon to go home and eat. But they were to return after eating, which they were only too glad to do because they were enjoying it.

All afternoon the dance continued. When the sun was going down they came out the last time. For this final dance Koshari showed them a new way. It consisted of an arm motion, as if pushing something aside. "Always use this when you finish your dances," he said.

Iatiku also attended the dance. She was pleased and thought that this public dance was a fine thing. When it was over Country Chief made a talk. "Koshari has made this dance for us. This is the way we're to have pleasure." Thanking Koshari, he told him that he had done well and to go home.

Koshari replied, "Yes, any time you call me I'll come. But next time make a bigger drum and have a lot of rattles." Country Chief told the people to make bigger drums and more rattles.

45.

Iatiku wants more entertainment for her people. She teaches them the kick stick race, using magical prayer sticks that represent rain clouds. The Katsinas like this, and she institutes a second kick game using wooden balls.

Iatiku was pleased that her people were happy. But she wanted still more joy for them. She knew that the Flint Society medicine men had a prayer stick which represented the power that makes the Clouds move. She decided to borrow it and have the men dance with it.

She told Flint Man to make this stick and pray to the Clouds to invite the Katsinas for their pleasure. They needed enjoyment, too, she thought. Flint Man did so and gave the prayer stick to Iatiku, who turned it over to Country Chief, who then chose some men to run a race.

Iatiku taught them how to do this. They were to kick the stick along, never touching it with their hands. First they were to head north, then turn left towards the west, then south, then back to the east to the plaza where the race began.

In came the Clouds bearing the Katsinas so they could watch this race. And afterwards it rained. The Clouds always travel with two of these kick sticks made of oak, one with a black stripe down the middle, the other all white. Flint Man and Country Chief waited at the goal. First to reach the plaza was the winner.

So Country Chief took one of the sticks and Flint Man the other. Carrying them to the arroyos they prayed with them. They found that this was a good game. As expected, it brought rain.

Flint Man also saw that the Katsinas had enjoyed it and were glad it had rained. So the men began practicing among themselves. Flint Man taught the runners how to train for it.

In April they were to take leaves from hardwood and make a tea, then tickle their throats with eagle down so they would vomit. But the medicinal tea would stay inside and make them strong and hardy like that tree. All their possessions they would bet on the race: blue, white, and black blankets, etc. After this they ran over a fifteen-mile race course every afternoon.

Iatiku thought of another game because she wanted to use the balls which the Katsinas struck together to make thunder and lightning. When that happens, lightning shoots down and the rolling balls become thunder. This ball game was held in the central plaza. She had Country Chief tell the Katsinas that the next time they came to bring those balls. When they did, the Messenger Katsina gave them to Country Chief as a present and taught him the game. This was also a gambling game. One turquoise bead was bet on a game. The people found the game very interesting. It was their first game of chance.

46.

The people move to White House, where the younger men begin gambling in the kivas and singing about women. Some prefer this to Iatiku's ceremonies. She is upset and decides to leave. She instructs Country Chief to take the remaining objects in her basket and establish Ha'ako Pueblo. She promises to greet her children at the end of their lives.

Iatiku told the people to leave Shipapu for the south. "You'll increase and scatter out," she said. So they moved and settled down at White House. After the people increased they were not sure how many there were. It was the business of Country Chief to know this, so he asked Iatiku how to count. She taught him by spreading her fingers. Beginning with the little finger on her left hand she named the first ten numbers.

At White House the men invented a game to play in the kiva. Duplicating the kick sticks, they carved four of them. They were hollow at one end and a pebble was hidden in one. Two teams were chosen. The team holding the sticks sang a song, the other team guessed which stick held the pebble. A couple of referees held a hundred straws, which were used as counters. The side to get all the straws won.

Some of the old men objected, saying that they had not been instructed to create this game. Iatiku did not like it either. The young men made up new songs to accompany the game, songs about women and referring humorously to other men's wives. They became more interested in playing this game in the kiva than in attending ceremonies. Things got worse until finally their songs were making fun of Iatiku.

Country Chief warned them to stop. When he was around they pretended to do so. But as soon as he was gone they resumed the games and songs. Some of the boys said that gambling was a better way of acquiring something they wanted than Iatiku's ceremonies.

This angered her. "All right," she said, "I'll let you live on your own and see for yourselves whether or not it's due to my instructions that all has been going well." From now on, she said, she would be quiet. They would hear from her no more.

First she told Country Chief, "You've made me cry. I feel hurt that I can no longer be with my people." Iatiku wanted him to watch over them. Even if they made fun of her ways she would remain their mother. She was going to Shipapu where she would wait for them to return to her at the end of their lives.

This was the first mention of death.

"It's been ordered that these two eggs which remain in the basket should be taken by the people until they reach a place called Ha'ako [the name for Acoma today]," she said. "It lies towards the south direction. Wherever the echo returns the clearest, they're to search there and call out, Ha'ako, Ha'ako! Where the sound returns best will be the right place. When you find this place you're to break an egg. One is parrot, the other is crow." She told them to break what they thought was the parrot egg at Ha'ako and to take the other one farther south.

Then she left.

47.

The people are on their own. The Katsinas and the
supernaturals of the four directions abandon them
as well. Drought and famine take over the land.
Country Chief gives one good man four days to
beg the Katsinas to save them.

Iatiku and her husband were gone. The people realized that
they had been wrong. The Katsinas and the rulers of the directions learned this as well. "Well, let it go at that," said
the Katsinas. "See if they can run the world by themselves.
We'll have our father [Antelope Man] there. We'll let them
alone for a while and not visit."

Spring came and it was dry. No clouds appeared. The
harvest was short. Country Chief went to pray to Iatiku to
come back. He made prayer sticks for the Katsinas, and Antelope Man did the same. They also prayed to the Kopishtaiya, who bring the seeds of all plants.

The medicine men worked as hard as they could. They set
up altars and made prayer sticks and prayed. But many seasons passed and they heard nothing from the gods. Everything dried up and famine came. The game animals were
hidden and hunters returned empty. Each year things got
increasingly scarce, although Country Chief told the people
to gather all the food they could. The boys stopped their
joking and took part in the prayers. Nothing seemed to
help. The people had lost their power.

At this time there was living a man by the name of Tsaiaiduit. He was a good and quiet man and never mixed with
other people. He was like a hermit, living by himself with
his mother. He was careful and saving with his crops. He
gathered grain without wasting any and picked up any he
found on the ground. Country Chief exhausted every other
way to call the Katsinas, so he thought of him.

When he visited Tsaiaiduit he discovered him to be the only person who still held some provisions. "I've come, my son, to get your help," Country Chief said. "I know you don't mix much with the people. But you believe in Iatiku. You were always first in prayers and made your offerings faithfully. I know that you take care of yourself in these things.

"I want you to call the Clouds," he said. "Maybe something will work for you and someone will listen. Maybe your prayers are stronger than ours. You've seen that we've tried and failed."

"I'm just a common human," he replied. "I've no power and nothing to give." But his mother spoke up. "Why don't you listen to him? It may be that the one-that-gives-us-life [Iatiku] will listen to you. We'll depend on your prayers."

"I don't know that I have power," the man said. "But my mother has asked me to do what you wish." Country Chief brought him sacred corn meal, prayer sticks, corn pollen, beads, tobacco. Country Chief prayed first, then told the man to pray with them. "Now it's up to you," said Country Chief. "I can only name the different kivas and the medicine."

Tsaiaiduit asked how many days were set aside for this. "Four days to prepare," Country Chief responded. "When the sun rises the fourth day you're to try." With that Country Chief left him alone.

48.

The solitary man seeks assistance from a Flint Society healer. The two go into isolation, purify themselve, and pray. Then the man dances in public until the rain returns to White House and the famine ends.

The man felt helpless and sorry for himself. But soon light came to his mind. He knew a medicine man of the Flint altar who was a quiet person like himself. He went to him and said, "Power has been given to you, and I ask for your help." The Flint medicine man had compassion and said, "Even I, who've been given power like the other curers, can do nothing. But I'll get myself together and help you."

He asked if Tsaiaiduit wanted help from the other medicine men of that altar. "No, just yourself," Tsaiaiduit replied. "All right," said the medicine man, "I'll help."

First he had Tsaiaiduit go to North Mountain. "Cut willows which are still green, also cut spruce branches." Teaching him a song, he had him sing it when he reached the mountain and was gathering the spruce. Tsaiaiduit did as told and brought the branches back.

The medicine man was waiting at Tsaiaiduit's house. "This is where you're going to work," he said. The Flint altar was already up. At the door the medicine man took the materials, making a path for him with his corn meal. "Tomorrow we'll purify ourselves by vomiting the medicine," he said.

They stayed apart from the people. Country Chief helped by keeping watch and guarding the house. All the while Tsaiaiduit's mother was encouraging him. The next day they made prayer sticks. After praying to Iatiku, they prayed to the North. Every time they made the sticks they purified themselves. They offered prayer sticks to the West, then to West Mountain, and to the other powers in that direction.

Thus they worked, one entire day for each different direction. After four days they had prayed to all the powers. Every night they sang, and every night Country Chief watched over the house until the singing was over. The people knew what was going on. All were helping with their prayers.

When the sun rose the fourth day, Tsaiaiduit dressed like the Katsina Tsaiaiduit, but without the mask. He created his own outfit. He had already been named after this Katsina, hence the attire.

Then Country Chief and the other officers brought him out—first to the north, then to the west, south, and east. Before he left his mother gave him words of encouragement. Tsaiaiduit danced and sang on each side of the plaza. The medicine men stayed in the house, singing the same as he sang outside.

He was a good singer and dancer. This was a song he sang during the famine.

Rain clouds come out.
Rain clouds come out.
Go, go upon the land.
The corn plant maiden
Stands beautifully upon the land.
Above, the clouds have formed.
Rain clouds come out.
Rain clouds, rain clouds come out.
Go, go upon the land.
The vine-plant maiden
Lies beautifully.
Above, the fog has formed.
From the west, the rain god comes together.
Let us go now, now.
I am going to make an offering.
I am going to offer for rain.
Here from the west,
The rain god messenger comes together.
Let us go now.
I am going to make an offering,
I am going to offer for rain.

Everyone came to see and support Tsaiaiduit. Many of the women cried in sympathy for him. But he was brave and did not slacken his singing or dancing until he had finished his four songs. While he was dancing Country Chief urged the people to stay with him and encourage him. Then Tsaiaiduit was escorted back to his house to rehearse four more songs.

When he came out a second time a small cloud appeared in the south. Iatiku and the Katsinas felt sorry for him. They had seen him working alone and decided to answer his prayers.

As he danced the cloud began to grow. By the time he had moved to the south side it began to rain hard. But Country Chief would not let the people go home.

Even in the rain Tsaiaiduit kept on dancing. After finishing his second dance, he was escorted back home to eat and break his fast. It was still raining when he came out the third time and the people stayed on. He returned and came out a fourth time. For four days and four nights it continued to rain. Country Chief thanked him and prayed over him as he released him from his duties.

Even today it is believed that the common people are the last resort and have the most power. If something bad should happen and the medicine men cannot help, the only hope will come from a common man.

PART TWO

BIRTH OF
THE WAR TWINS

49.

While the people are still at White House, a woman and daughter are treated as outcasts. The girl goes picking piñon nuts and meets Sun Youth, ruler of the sun. He gives her two piñons to eat and she becomes pregnant. Back home her magical basket continues to produce piles of piñons.

After the famine at White House there was a woman living with her daughter. Everyone hated them. They looked after their own field and no one spoke to them or invited them to their house. But the Katsinas were fond of them, as they always made offerings to them.

It was customary for the people to gather prickly pears, piñons, and yucca fruit. One season there were plenty of piñons, so the daughter asked her mother if she could get some. But her mother worried, "There's no one to look after you." The girl insisted, saying she could go alone.

She took a lunch and followed the other people. When she arrived at their camp no one asked her over, so she camped alone. She passed the night and the next day went out alone.

At noon suddenly somebody stood before her. He was Sun Youth, the spirit and ruler of the Sun. "Are you picking piñons?" he asked. "Yes," she answered, "but you frightened me." Sun said, "I'll help you pick piñons. I've brought you two. I want you to eat them." "Who are you?" she asked. "I'm the Sun," he answered. "Where do you live?" she asked. "Where the sun rises," he answered. She thanked him for the piñons.

After he left she ate the piñons and became pregnant. He had promised to help her, so whenever she picked piñons they increased in her basket. Seeing that she had more than she could carry she decided to return home. But when she put the load on her back it was lighter.

At home her mother praised her. "You certainly have gathered lots of piñons." The other people were drying their piñons on the roofs of their houses, so they did the same. When they spilled out of her basket the piñons grew into a large pile. The mother and girl were astonished at how many.

The girl told her mother how Sun Youth had promised to help. She also said he had given her the two piñons to eat, and maybe that explained what had happened. She did not know she was to have children from them.

50.

The girl gives birth to two boys, Masewi and Oyoyewi. They grow rapidly and like to hunt. Their grandmother makes them bows and arrows.

Time passed and her condition became noticeable. Her mother saw and asked if she were pregnant. She said no, since she knew that she had met no man. Other people saw as well. Soon she gave birth to two children.

After four days they were presented to the Sun and given names. Masewi was the older, and Oyoyewi, the younger. She wondered how she had gotten that way. Then she remembered eating the two piñons from Sun Youth.

The babies were small and not handsome. But they grew rapidly. Soon they were crawling. Before long they began to walk. They started to speak early. Soon they were leaving the house, and were never afraid. Their grandmother warned them not to go too far from the village lest animals get them, but they did not listen.

The twins would wander off and stay away all day. They grew fond of hunting, starting with birds and rabbits. When they came home they described the animals they had seen. They spoke of seeing one with horns and asked if it was something to eat. Their grandmother said it was a jack rabbit. They tried to catch it, but it ran too fast, so they asked how to kill it.

"I'll make you something to kill it with," their grandmother said. She had an old round winnowing basket she no longer used. She pulled the bent stick out of the basket's rim and cut it in two. Using sinew she tied the ends of the two parts together. Giving one of these bows to each boy, she said, "This is a bow." She took the name from the word for "rainbow."

Then she took some stirring sticks from the bundle used for stirring corn meal batter. "You're to use these with the bow," she said. "They're arrows." She showed them how to shoot with them.

51.

Their father, the Sun, secretly helps the boys be-come good hunters. They tease a bear and her cubs. Then they kill it and plan to give the paws to the medicine men.

.

The boys took their new weapons out to hunt. Their father, the Sun, was always watching and helping them. It was he who made them grow fast and mature quickly. Now he wanted to see how they used their new bows and arrows.

When they saw a rabbit they crawled up to it and shot. Although the arrow just touched the rabbit, it fell over any-way. They ran up and caught it. It was by the power of the Sun that they did this. They took the rabbit home, and their grandmother and mother were pleased. Happy with their success the boys were eager for more hunting.

Sometimes they played with other children, but they were mean and stronger and made the others cry. They preferred to go alone into the countryside to hunt. With the Sun's help they began to kill larger animals. They easily found deer and antelope, for the Sun made these animals come to them.

The large animals they killed were too heavy to carry, so they returned for their grandmother. She feared the boys would wander too far and tried scaring them by saying that lions and bears would carry them off. Each time she named a new fierce animal, they went looking for it.

They kept their grandmother busy making buckskin. Soon they were killing even bigger animals like lions and bears, and kept her making rugs from their hides.

Once their grandmother told them the bear would eat them, so they went to see if that was true. They invented a stick if the bear proved dangerous. Sharpening a piece of hardwood at both ends, they said, "With this we will over-power you."

They came upon two cubs and started playing with them. They ran around until the cubs whined. Then the cubs cried as the boys poked sticks in their eyes. The boys kept watch for the mother bear and soon they heard her.

She charged, but the boys stood their ground. Masewi was in front. As the bear bit at him he thrust the two-pointed stick into her mouth. The bear stopped and pawed at its bloody mouth while the boys stood by and laughed. It was fun for them. After they laughed as much as they wanted, they killed her.

Their grandmother had told them that medicine men used bear paws, so they thought they would cut them off as presents for them. This is how Koshari would have done it, too. But bear paws used by the medicine men in their ceremonies are not supposed to be taken this way.

52.

The boys set out to find their father. The Sun sends Spider Woman to show them how to travel. They descend into her home and fall asleep. She has Spider Boy give them protective medicine and places them in a basket, which she drops near the Sun's house.

After they grew a little older the boys heard other children speak about their fathers. They went to their mother and asked why they didn't have someone to know as a father. She told them he did not live here. The boys asked where he lived and she said at the place where the sun rises.

How far was that, they asked, and how many sunrises before they could reach it? She didn't know, only that it was the place where the sun came up. They asked if they could go visit him. But she said they could never get there, so there was no use trying. She didn't think they would leave.

They always rose early before sunrise and prayed, for they were well taught in religious practices. When they got up the next morning they talked together and decided to go to their father. When the sun came up, they said, "It's not far, just on the other side of the mountain." They started walking fast. But when they reached the crest of the first range they saw other mountains as far away as the first had been.

Then someone spoke to them. It was Spider Woman. "My children," she said, "are you going to visit your father?" They were startled. "Did someone speak?" they said. "Who is it? Who are you?" Spider Woman answered, "Here I am." They looked towards the voice and saw a spider on a bush. "Is that you, Spider Woman? Do you speak?" "Yes," she replied.

The boys told her they were going to visit their father. She said not to go just yet, to wait until the next day. Sun already knew they were coming and had sent her to instruct them how to reach him.

Spider Woman had the boys follow her. Reaching her house, she said, "Come on down." They saw her go in and asked how they could fit through such a small hole. "Put your foot in," she said. "It'll be large enough." The older boy stepped in, the hole got larger, and he could see a stairway. As he descended he called to his brother, "Come on, it's large enough." When they reached the bottom there was a room with many young spiders crawling around the walls. They were afraid of the boys.

Spider Woman fed them. She had only one boy in her family, so she asked him to collect webs from the other spiders and spin them into a ball so as to reach to the house of Sun Man. When her son finished Spider Woman told the boys to rest. They were to start right after midnight.

At midnight Spider Woman woke Masewi and Oyoyewi. She told Spider Boy to get a small basket made of spider web, put the two boys in it, and take them to their father's house. He'd guide them all the way.

As she held one end of the ball of spun web, Spider Boy dropped down with the other end. The web unwound as he went. Soon the two boys became completely lost, but they didn't worry.

Before the sun rose they reached their destination. Spider Boy took them out of the basket and asked Masewi to let him crawl behind his ear so he could talk to him. For their protection he gave the boys some medicine roots to chew and rub on their bodies.

"I'll come to advise you," said Spider Boy. "You'll spit towards the House where the Sun lives." The Sun already knew that his sons were coming, and told his sisters to wait for them.

5 3 ·

In his kiva the boys meet their father. The Sun and his brothers put them in a mountain lion's den. When they emerge unharmed, they are put with wolves, then with lynx, and then with bees. Nothing happens to them. Finally the boys are thrown into the kiva, which provides the sun's heat. Instead of burning up they emerge as full-grown men.

Arriving at the bottom of the house the boys began climbing its ladder. When the Sun's sisters saw them they said, "Two boys are coming up. They look poor and dirty." One said, "Maybe they're our brother's sons." The others replied, "That can't be. Our brother's children would be better cared for."

When the boys reached the top they walked right in, just like Koshari, without any ceremony. Sun Youth had his own kiva. One of the women told him that the two boys had arrived. "Maybe they're your sons," she said. "Come up and see them."

Upon entering the boys asked for their father. By then Sun Youth was already there and said, "My sons, you've come." He picked them up and carried them down into the kiva. "My sons have come," he told his brothers, who were also inside.

"Are these the kind of sons you have?" they laughed. One asked if they were really his. "If that's so put them in the north den with the mountain lions and see if they come out alive."

Their father took them to the lions. But the boys were used to them and unafraid. Soon the animals were acting friendly, licking and playing. One man went to see if the boys were eaten. "No, they're playing together," he reported. So they were taken out.

"Put them in the west den with the wolves," the man said. "They're always hungry." Again the boys came out alive. The same happened when they were placed with the lynx in the

south den. And when they were put in the east den with the
bumblebees, the bees swarmed all over them.

As one boy opened his mouth a bee got in. He bit it and told
his brother, "They're good. They taste sweet." They gathered
others, breaking them open and sucking out the honey. When
the man came to check on them he saw the boys were unharmed and released them. They had killed a lot of their bees,
he said.

In that kiva was a special hollow filled with burning coals,
which was where the sun got its heat. Other kivas have their
altars in this same spot. Now they gave the boys a final test,
grabbing them and throwing them in. Instead of being burned,
they came out as full-grown men, and as good-looking as their
father.

54.

The boys are given bows and arrows and staffs of office. They were also given powerful rabbit-hunting sticks so as to represent the sun. They learn how to bring what they kill back to life. They are clothed with handsome regalia and their faces are painted to make them brave.

Everyone was convinced the boys were truly the Sun's children. They agreed to return them to the people the next day. In the meantime they would make them more handsome.

The boys had brought their bows and arrows. Now the men improved them, putting sinew backs on the bows and shaping them better. To the arrows they added stone points and feathers and quivers of mountain lion skin to hold them. They also fashioned staffs for them and declared that now they would be Country Chiefs. The staffs fit into a special pocket in the quivers. With them they would be strong and protected.

The boys were told that, as representatives of the Sun, they would be powerful rulers. So their father also made them a curved rabbit stick. They must only use it when necessary, for it held so much power it could be destructive. If they killed something and felt sorry about it, they could place one of their staffs or an arrowhead on the body and it would come back to life.

Their father also made them eight arrows. One bunch of four were for hunting, the other four were only for emergencies. The boys would be allowed to go everywhere, he said, to the North, South, West, and East, even to the most sacred places. Wherever they went they would be heeded. "Whenever you want to come back to my house," he said, "the doors will be open to you."

Their father gave them beaded moccasins, girdle, sash,

and arm bands decorated with feathers. He added wrist bands made of buffalo skin, which they must wear for their protection. They must never take them off, for their hearts were in them. He also gave them necklaces of turquoise and shell beads.

"With all of these you'll look handsome and have power to attract," he said. He painted red around their eyes, saying, "This is the way you'll paint up for bravery."

55.

The boys are given headdresses and pouches containing fetishes. The next morning their father shows them the world and answers their questions. With Spider Boy they travel in the basket back to Spider Woman's house. Now they are grown men and continue to live in the village as common people.

All this time Spider was coaching them, telling them not to be afraid as they underwent the different tests. Their father made a special headdress for them to hang on the back of their hair, and a pouch on a strap over their shoulders and across their chests. In it the Sun placed a number of fetishes, which they must carry always.

Finally Sun Youth looked them over. They appeared handsome. "I have given you all that you need for bravery, good luck, and power," he said. They were to stay overnight and return the following day, accompanying him and the sun. Spider Boy told them to agree. They were escorted from the kiva into the other room, given food, and there they spent the night.

The next day Sun Youth placed his sons high in the sky. The sun began to rise and appeared over the horizon. Their father was talking to them, pointing things out as they looked down. They asked many questions, so that nothing would puzzle them.

At last their father said, "Now we're near your house." Sun Youth knew how they had traveled and was aware that Spider Boy remained with them. Spider Boy put them in the hanging basket. Their father held the web's other end. The boys assured him that they would do all that he asked and follow his advice.

As before, the boys were lost, not knowing how far they traveled. They arrived at the house of Spider Woman and thanked her and said they had seen their father. After saying a prayer for her they departed and returned home.

Fearing they were lost or eaten by mountain lions, their grandmother and mother had been praying for them. They'd searched everywhere but couldn't find them. At first their mother didn't recognize them because they were good-looking grown men. Their grandmother hardly believed that they were the same boys. They told how they'd met their father and how he'd given them their names.

Then the grandmother and mother believed them. The boys removed their outfits and hung them up, for they'd been instructed not to wear them until they needed them. For themselves they now made ordinary clothing, and continued to live in the village as common people.

PART THREE

THE WAR TWINS' WORLD

56.

For a while peace returns to the people at White House. Then they begin gambling again. The Katsinas visit the village. When most of them depart, one Katsina hangs behind. He spies on people mocking the Katsinas and tells the rest. The Katsinas plan their revenge.

When the rains finally returned to White House they came too late and did not produce a large harvest. But they yielded a lot of wild food plants that the people gathered and prepared for the winter. The game animals also returned.

This was the reawakening of the Katsinas. Now they resumed visiting the people when they were asked. Whenever the Kopishtaiya were called, they showed up as well. The people continued to hold their pleasure dances and the games that were given them. For a long time they quit the gambling game.

All was going well until someone who had that game brought it back. Again the young people began to play, although the old folks scolded them. One time the Katsinas came to visit, bringing their presents and the rain. The night after they left, a Katsina lingered behind. The boys crowded into the kiva to play. This Katsina got inside without being noticed. Staying in back of the crowd he watched and overheard their talking and singing.

A gambler got fresh and sang a song which became disrespectful. Some men started to dance like Katsinas. They made fun of them and mocked some of their peculiarities— imitating the ones with bow-legs and off-set lips. One boy joked, "Is this the way the clouds look?"

So the Katsina left and called out to the other Katsinas. When the people overheard his voice from outside the kiva they were startled. "Who was that who left?" they wondered. Someone said they thought they'd noticed a real Katsina step out. Now the people grew frightened. "A Katsina has seen us mock the Katsinas," they said.

One man was just entering the kiva when he ran into this Katsina on the roof. Once inside he asked, "What was that Katsina doing here?" Now the people were certain that they'd made a mistake and got quiet. They felt heavy-hearted and quit playing and went home.

When this Katsina returned to Wenimats he yelled and the rest of the Katsinas became excited and rushed out. They overheard when he reported to Katsina Chief what he'd seen. Even before he was finished some grew angry. Katsina Chief tried pacifying them, "Wait, don't get excited." But Messenger Katsina took their side. "I'm going to tell the people that we're coming to visit them," he declared. Katsina Chief told him not to go, but he left anyway. Katsina Chief pleaded for calm. He wanted to settle the matter by discussion, if possible, without harming anyone.

57.

After midnight Messenger Katsina informs the people that the Katsinas will soon arrive with presents. They notice something strange about his voice. When he shows up again he does not smile or joke and runs away from them.

Just after midnight the people heard Messenger Katsina from the plaza. "I've brought you some news," he announced. "The Katsinas are going to visit you with presents. They'll bring everything you need, hunting sticks, clubs. Wait for them, make prayer sticks, and prepare a feast."

Messenger Katsina gave a strange yell they'd never heard before. It sounded like crying. They were frightened and wondered why he seemed so different. The mockers from the kiva were the only ones to guess the reason. They knew their making fun must be the cause. No one went to bed. Everyone stayed awake and questioned one another.

Messenger Katsina left, but just before sun-up he returned. This second visit they saw the clubs and hunting sticks in his hands. Antelope Man painted himself and put on his full attire in which he always met the Katsinas. Country Chief and his officers did likewise, and all went forth to meet him.

Antelope Man asked, "Have you come, my son?" Messenger Katsina answered, "Yes, my father, I'm here to tell you that the Katsinas are anxious to come and visit. They'll arrive a little after noon. They're bringing presents for your people."

Everyone was watching. Antelope Man tried to talk with Messenger Katsina as usual, but he wouldn't come near. Antelope Man asked why he didn't step forward and explain why the Katsinas were coming. He asked Messenger Katsina to stop and offered him a cigarette.

But Messenger Katsina made excuses, saying he didn't want to smoke because tobacco made you lazy, your joints cracked, and your eyes watered so you couldn't see a deer when you went hunting. They tried other ways to coax him to stop and talk. But he was leading the angry Katsinas and wouldn't respond.

So Antelope Man asked Messenger Katsina to hand him the stick he carried. "Aren't you going to give it away?" he said. "You're my friend, why don't you give it to me?" Coming near and trying to calm him, Antelope Chief caught hold of him. But Messenger Katsina hit him with the club.

Other men jumped on Messenger Katsina and disarmed him. Antelope Man had him brought to the kiva, hoping they could humor him and quiet him down. When Messenger Katsina broke free they chased after him, but he was faster and got away.

58.

*The Katsinas attack the people at White House.
Using their rabbit-hunting clubs, the sons of the
Sun help the people kill the Katsinas. The surviv-
ing Katsina leader says both sides were wrong.
The fighting frightens the people.*

Messenger Katsina returned to Wenimats with another com-
plaint. They had seized his clubs and sticks. When he told
the others he exaggerated what had happened and persuaded
the Katsinas that the people were wicked. They became furi-
ous. Again the Katsina Chief tried to quiet them, but they
wouldn't listen and left in a large band.

The people living at White House knew something was
wrong. They got busy making prayer sticks and praying to
the Katsinas. Even though the prayer sticks reached the
Katsinas, they weren't accepted.

The Katsinas were on the war path. They ran right over
their leader. He was injured trying to stop them. Soon the
people heard them coming. They were yelling with the same
tone of voice that they'd heard from Messenger Katsina before. Country Chief called the men together and told them
to leave the Katsinas alone. "If they're going to harm us,"
he said, "let's do as they wish. Maybe this is our punishment. We've been behaving wrongly."

The Katsinas brought clubs, but they also picked up hardwood sticks and broken branches. As they approached the
village they did not pause but rushed in the back way, all in
a bunch. They began beating and killing everyone around.

The sons of the Sun were still living in the village as common men. They hadn't thought anything serious would happen, but they got angry as they saw people killed. Putting on
the outfits their father had given them they painted each other
as he'd instructed and gathered their bows and quivers.

So far no one attempted to defend themselves. The Twins headed for the largest cluster of Katsinas. They knew they weren't supposed to use their hunting sticks on ordinary occasions, but this time it was necessary. Giving out the yell their father taught them that drew power from the Sun, each threw their stick. The Katsinas that were grouped in the plaza were decapitated. The rest scattered in every direction.

The Twins killed the remaining Katsinas, except for their leader. Along with Country Chief, he'd tried to calm the Katsinas. They captured Messenger Katsina and scolded him. "Because of you our people have been killed. You're looking for trouble, so you will have it." They tied him down and castrated him. Recognizing the Twins from their prayers, Messenger Katsina pleaded, "Oh, it's you! Please forgive me!"

When Katsina Chief saw all the dead Katsinas he grew afraid. "I think we've done something wrong," he said, "else by whose power has this been done?" By that he meant that both sides were at fault.

This was the first time the people saw death.

The Twins stepped forward and said, "We're the ones. It had to be done. We stood up for the people. We understand the Katsinas are sacred to us. But it's also been held that the Katsinas should care for the people, too."

Everyone was terror-stricken. What had happened was mysterious. The people came out of hiding and gathered in the plaza with Country Chief, the Twins, Katsina Chief, and Messenger Katsina.

59.

The older twin makes peace with the Katsina leader. The Katsinas are restored to life. Both sides take responsibility. From now on the Katsinas will help people from afar. But they will teach people how to represent them. When the Twins fail to bring the people back to life, death is created, and the medicine men recall Iatiku's rites of burial.

Once the older twin finished explaining why they'd fought, Katsina Chief understood. When he realized that this twin was their father, Masewi, Katsina Chief came forward and embraced him. On behalf of all the Katsinas he confessed that they'd done wrong.

Country Chief spoke to Masewi. "You've performed this miracle," he said. "Why should this be so hard and serious. Forgive us all. For our sake can you bring the Katsinas back? We understand that it's by the Katsinas that we've lived and been happy."

The older twin turned to Katsina Chief and asked if this was true. If they brought the Katsinas back to life, however, there must be no more anger or killing. Katsina Chief said that he confessed on behalf of all of them, and agreed that Country Chief was right.

Masewi said, "I know that this should never have happened. We, too, feel sorry for the Katsinas, whom we've depended upon. We'll try to do what you've asked. If our power works, maybe they'll be with us again."

The Twins returned to the bodies of the Katsinas scattered on the ground. They picked up their severed heads. Their father the Sun had given them a special medicine herb called "jack-rabbit ears," which they rubbed on the necks of the Katsinas to connect their heads again. On their chests they placed their staffs with the arrowhead, much as they'd been shown how to bring the animals back to life.

Some Katsinas returned to life and became strong again. Others recovered more slowly. A few did not come back at all. The Twins worked over them through the day until sundown. Country Chief sent the people away while they were doing this, explaining that it wasn't good for them to watch what was happening. The medicine men helped, but all they really did was follow the Twins' instructions.

After doing their best and bringing back to life all they could, Country Chief confessed to the Katsinas that the trouble was their fault. Katsina Chief said the Katsinas also made a mistake, and were equally responsible.

To protect both sides Katsina Chief decided that the Katsina shouldn't come and visit anymore, or else they might get angry again. "You won't see us again," he said. "But we'll still help you from Wenimats. We'll always be waiting for you there. You've received the presents of our outfits and regalia. From now on you're going to imitate us. This is how we'll help you from there. You've seen how we're painted up and dressed. You know how to make our prayer sticks. Go through the ceremony like this and we'll help you spiritually. Whenever someone has chosen the dress of the particular Katsina they're to represent, his power will come and attach itself while they represent him."

"How can this be made real?" Country Chief asked. "We're not appointed to do this." And Katsina Chief replied, "I guess you'll have to be initiated. In this way you'll really represent the Katsinas." So Katsina Chief laid down the word that he would be called to teach them how to carry this out and initiate the people in learning how to be Katsinas.

Masewi asked if this was all, and Katsina Chief said, "Yes." But Masewi replied, "This isn't over for you yet. You must receive punishment. You'll fast for three tens of the times the sun comes up. At the end of that you'll all become really reborn. When this is done we'll regard you as we have before." The elder twin also said that at the end of this time he would come with his brother to Wenimats.

Everyone felt bad and sorry for each other. They came together and the people brought prayer sticks to the Katsinas. Both sides confessed their wrongdoing and said prayers for each other.

The Katsinas departed. When they returned to Wenimats they all died again. For these thirty days they were barely alive enough to realize their punishment. During this time Katsina Chief looked after them.

Now Country Chief asked the Twins if they could bring the people back to life. "Yes, we can," they answered. All the bodies were carried into the plaza. With them the Twins performed as they had with the Katsinas. But none of them came to life. The Twins had made a mistake.

Their father had seen what they'd done. After they'd finished with the Katsinas he took away the powers of their medicine staffs, their arrowheads, and their hunting sticks. This is why they couldn't bring the people back to life.

"Well, we've failed," said Masewi and Oyoyewi. "What's to be done now?" Country Chief and the medicine men said it had been laid down that if anything like this happened certain rules must be followed. "Iatiku said that at some time we'd come to the end of life. Maybe this is what's happened."

So followed the first funeral ritual. The medicine men painted the faces of the dead men and women. They remembered how Iatiku showed them the sand painting of the figure of the earth, with the head to the east. They thought that probably meant the body should be returned to the earth with the head in that direction—and the feet pointed where the sun goes down. This is the way the medicine men planted the bodies of the people, so they would be reborn. In burials the word "plant" is used in this sense.

60.

Quarrel and strife return. Anticipating an angry reaction from the Katsinas, some bands of people go away. When two Katsinas do come back they teach the people how to use masks, feathers, paint, and self-purification so they can initiate new members into the Katsina Society.

After this the people began quarreling among themselves. They found new bad words to use against each other. Fights and feuds arose. They no longer liked each other.

They'd heard the talk between Country Chief and Katsina Chief. They knew Katsina Chief said he was coming back to teach the people how to act in the supernatural manner of the Katsinas. But some were still afraid. They thought that if they made a mistake and didn't fast and behave just right they'd pay with their lives.

Others believed everything would be all right. "Let's do as we're asked," they said. "We'll learn to carry on as they want us to."

Some people didn't want to see that day come and packed up and left in small bands, or perhaps just a man and his wife went away. It is not known where they went, but they were never heard from again. Those willing to take instructions from Katsina Chief stayed.

Everyone waited for when the Katsinas would return. Each day they made a tally mark until they got to the three tens. When the thirtieth day approached, Antelope Man called the people. He told them what he and Katsina Chief had discussed—that the Katsinas would be reborn and the people would help in their rebirth and still believe in them.

They made prayer sticks and brought them to Antelope Man's altar. He took them and prayed to the Katsinas and invited them to visit. When the thirty days were up, Masewi and

Oyoyewi went to Wenimats. With their prayers they gave new life to the Katsinas. As they arrived on the mountain above Wenimats they cried out, "All clouds in the north, all clouds in the west, all clouds in the south, all clouds in the east—all that have been asleep all this time. Come awake!"

So the Katsinas awoke. And the Kopishtaiya and Koshari and the rulers of the four directions who had been asleep in Wenimats woke up as well. The clouds had rested because they had no one to pray to them while the Katsinas slept. Thus all awoke in good health.

Antelope Man's prayer sticks had arrived and Katsina Chief accepted them. The rest of the Katsinas took them, too, and prayed to the people and smoked cigarettes to re-establish contact. But Katsina Chief warned that they weren't to visit the village anymore.

He had Messenger Katsina tell the people that on the fourth day he'd come by himself to initiate them—to give them the strength and the right to act the Katsina way. He carried that message and was in a good humor when he informed the people that Katsina Chief would arrive by himself in four days. They were to wait and purify themselves and prepare a feast. Everyone understood that they were going to be initiated.

On the fourth day Katsina Chief appeared. Antelope Man's altar was prepared for him. Messenger Katsina came, too, with lots of feather down. Everyone entered the kiva with them.

The singing began. One at a time the people were brought up. While Messenger Katsina held them, the Katsina Chief struck each one four times with the yucca leaves. Then he tied a feather down on their heads.

They were instructed by Katsina Chief how to make masks, duplicating the ones they had seen the rest of the Katsinas wearing. "You've seen their feathers," he said. "You know how they're painted and how they wear their attire. You'll do the same and carry this on into the future as long as there is life."

They were to fast four days, eight days, or twelve days, according to what they were doing. During these days they were not to touch a woman. For four days they were to fast and purify their systems by vomiting. On the fourth day they were to pray to Wenimats.

Still fasting, on the fifth day they were to bring their masks to the kiva. Then they should compose new dance songs and paint the masks and make new regalia. On the eighth day the people representing Katsinas would come out and dance a day and a half. The following day they were to be sent back to Wenimats. From then on, eight days more fasting. No mixing with people, and no touching of women.

All this was laid down as rules. Everyone understood them. Some were satisfied with this, but others were not. They'd been too afraid to participate and were left with no power.

61.

The people make their Katsina masks from buf-
falo hide. With their prayer sticks and altars the
medicine men give life to the masks. Only the initi-
ated know about this. Now people experience the
powers of the particular Katsina they represent.

After all this Antelope Man wanted to see how it would work. So the men who were willing to take part met in the kiva. Country Chief taught them to make masks, saying that they still must be brought to life before they could be used. "The mask you make will belong to you," he explained. "Name it for whatever Katsina you represent."

They tried using different skins. Those made of buckskin didn't look good and had to be made over. The best masks were of tough, heavy buffalo hide. It took a long time to make this first set. Some made funny masks, but they persisted. Some laughed at those who could not make them. Many got discouraged and left.

They sewed the buffalo skin in the shape of a mask. They found it best to fill them with dry earth, then tamp them down for a smooth shape. It took a while to dry them. Next they had to paint them, but they did not know where to find the paint. They had to do a lot of experimenting before they were finished. But they could do anything with them because they were not yet sacred.

As best they could they fixed them to look like the particular Katsina they had chosen. They helped one another and in this way some got finished. "The rest will be up to our fathers, the medicine men," they said. "They're the ones who know better what to do now."

Those taking part made prayer sticks for Country Chief to present to the medicine men and seek their assistance. After he visited the Flint and Fire medicine men, they accepted the sticks. On the fourth night they promised to help bring the masks to life so they could truly represent the Katsinas.

All awaited the coming of the fourth day. During this time the medicine men prepared their altars. The men who'd made the masks waited in the kiva. Then they received word to bring them to various altars.

The medicine men went through their ceremonies. Just as they'd done with the fetishes, they gave life to the masks. Each one was named for the particular Katsina that they represented. Only the medicine men witnessed this.

When the medicine men finished giving life to a mask, they blew it with sacred breath towards the owner. Then they gave it to him. Each time they said, "This is now real and has the same power as the real Katsina. You must take good care of it and not neglect it. Most of all, this is going to be secret from this day on. Children and those who are not initiated must not know about this. They must not know that the dancers are not real Katsinas. Only women who have become grandmothers shall know of this."

When all was done, Antelope Man said, "Let's try it out. Get to work and prepare." He had the men follow Katsina Chief's rules and procedures. So they did and on the fourth day entered the kiva for the first time. They made the prayer sticks with which to summon the power of the real Katsinas whom they were to represent.

62.

A man impersonating a Katsina prays to Messenger Katsina that he may be like him. Wearing his mask and attire he enters the plaza. After him come the other impersonators, all singing. At first some people are afraid the Katsinas are coming to fight them again. They greet the procession with sacred corn meal and lead them to the kiva.

For four days and nights the people composed songs similar to those the Katsinas had sung. In every way they tried to imitate the Katsinas, singing and dancing like them. Except they did this without masks or painting up. By the fourth day all had gone well.

In the morning they sent out the man who was to represent Messenger Katsina. He took his mask concealed in his blanket. He also carried paint. Accompanying and guarding him was an officer of Country Chief. Out in the country, where no one could see him, he dressed and painted himself in the image of Messenger Katsina.

With him were two prayer sticks he had made. Placing the mask before him and facing it west towards Wenimats, he prayed. "I'm praying to the real Messenger Katsina," he said. "I've made a mask which looks like you. I know you're giving it your power. So I also ask that the power of your body and mind be placed in my body and mind. Even though I'm a common human and you're real, help me represent you as you would like me to—help me to do it really."

As he slipped the mask over his head he said, "You that are real, clothe me!" Delivering Messenger Katsina's cry, he said, "Now I hope to represent you so that my people may go on believing in the Katsinas." Then he headed towards the village, singing.

It was sunrise when Messenger Katsina arrived at the pueblo.

The War Chief's helper, who was guarding him, kept out of sight. Then he entered the plaza. Of course, Country Chief, Antelope Man, and the medicine men knew he was coming. Just as he'd done with the real Katsinas, Antelope Man went through the welcoming ritual. The other officials welcomed him as well.

This Messenger Katsina notified them that all the different kinds of Katsinas were coming. While he was still in the plaza, the other impersonators were hidden out in the countryside. As they put on their masks and outfits each prayed to the particular Katsina they represented. They were also talking just like the Katsinas. Then they headed towards the pueblo, all singing.

Soon the people heard them. The children and the uninitiated grew afraid and unsure whether the Katsinas were coming to kill again. They trembled from their recollections. Country Chief cried out that the Katsinas were only visiting. Everyone should quit playing and be polite and pay attention.

When the Katsinas came in sight all the people, as was customary, brought out sacred corn meal and made a path for them into the pueblo. They spoke prayers that they made up themselves. Antelope Man went forth to greet them using the same words he'd used when greeting the real Katsinas.

Welcoming them into the plaza he led them in a row to the north side, where they always danced first. Already the officers had prepared things for them in the kiva where they would rest afterwards.

They danced the Katsina dance. All was done in direct imitation of the real Katsinas. Four times they danced—in the north, the west, the south, and the east. Afterwards they were led into the kiva to rest.

63.

The Katsina impersonators emerge from the kiva to dance and sing some more. They are fed and offered prayer sticks. Once they leave the village each of them prays to his Katsina to be released, so they all can return home as ordinary human beings once again.

On the kiva's west side the skins of different animals were laid out to form a bench—skins from lion, buffalo, or bear. Taking off their masks, the dancers placed them here. Country Chief and his officers had tobacco ready and gave every dancer a smoke. They prepared their songs. Each time they put on the masks to go out again, they repeated the words they'd said before. This second round in the plaza they danced four more times.

About midday they returned to the kiva. Country Chief announced that the people should also go home to rest, and not reappear until the Katsinas came out again. The old women who knew that the dancers were actually men brought their food. When they entered Antelope Man stood up and offered the food first to the real Katsinas [who were not there], then to the masks resting on the bench. Since midnight the dancers had not been allowed to drink or eat. Now they could break their fast.

While still in the kiva the old women selected which masked Katsinas to hand presents to, asking them to give them, in turn, to specific households. After the third dance they distributed the gifts as requested. By the time they left the kiva for the fourth time the sun was setting. The dancers presented the people with more things. Then the dance was over.

Antelope Man told everyone to bring prayer sticks and place them in a basket in the plaza. This basket he presented to Messenger Katsina to take with him. When the fourth and last dance was done the masked dancers made presents just as the real Katsinas had done. They removed their attire, except for their masks, and presented them to members of their own households, or to women who knew about them, so they would be able to retrieve them later. As they disposed of their clothes, one by one these Katsinas ran off over the desert. They were shouting, but their sounds grew fainter and fainter. They strung out and disappeared in the distance, accompanied by Messenger Katsina and the prayer sticks.

When they reached the place where they were to unmask, they only lifted the masks halfway—just over the eyes. Taking some prayer sticks they went off by themselves to pray. "Now, I believe that you've finished your work," each one said to his particular Katsina. "Go back happily to Wenimats! Take with you all that belongs to you and everything that's sacred to you. Don't trouble me by your power returning to haunt me in my dreams."

Each one took off his mask and motioned four times towards Wenimats. "Let me return to my people like a common human," they said. "Don't blame me for what I've been doing. Let nothing wrong happen because I've imitated you. Let me have good health, long life, and the gifts you've brought."

They buried the prayer sticks. Taking the feathers from their masks, they put them in shape to carry home. Waiting until dark they scattered out again and returned to the village, one at a time, from different directions. They went to the kiva to turn in the masks.

Antelope Man thanked the men who'd taken part. All had gone well, he said. But they must not have sexual relations for eight days yet. These were the instructions to Antelope Man from the real Katsina Chief. If anyone broke these rules, even after undergoing all this hardship, he wouldn't receive the blessings for which he had prayed. He might even shorten his life and die.

64.

The rains resume. Next the people decide to impersonate the winter Katsinas. They run hard and become tough and care for their masks. That winter there is a lot of snow and good hunting.

After this all went well at White House. It began raining and continued at frequent intervals. During that summer and fall the people had plenty of everything.

In the winter Antelope Man thought of trying out the Kopishtaiya to help the people. Country Chief announced they should make prayer sticks to call them. After vomiting for four days to purify themselves the men taking part met in the kiva. Again they made prayer sticks and prepared masks. For four days they worked. The songs they made were different from Katsina songs. They were not for dancing but for manliness.

Then the impersonators painted up, picked up their masks and outfits, and left at midnight. They went east, into the country and away from people. Country Chief told everyone that on the fourth day they were to expect the Kopishtaiya to arrive from that direction.

These Kopishtaiya impersonators got ready just as the Katsina ones had done. But they were painted differently, had different feathers, and their prayer sticks were made of hardwood to represent masculinity. In pairs they hid in various places where they dressed and prayed and asked the real Kopishtaiya to assist them. They adopted the yell and accent of the particular Kopishtaiya they represented. They were told to be sure to approach the pueblo in pairs and to gather just before sun-up.

It was cold. As soon as they were dressed they began running to keep warm. Arriving near the pueblo before sunrise they all entered together, but still as pairs. As before Antelope Man opened the road for them with sacred corn meal.

When the real Kopishtaiya first came they brought all kinds of evergreen trees. They left them in the plaza for the people to make tea and purify themselves. Some men displayed their manliness by carrying spiny cactus on their backs; others held big chunks of cold ice in their arms. These Kopishtaiya also got real snow to scatter around.

Just before sunrise the Kopishtaiya impersonators were led in. They planted all they'd brought and distributed seeds to the people. They scattered cactus fluff to represent snow. Anyone desiring bravery and manliness squeezed up against the Kopishtaiya with the cactus. They broke pieces from the evergreen boughs, to boil them at home and purify themselves. As soon as the sun appeared these Kopishtaiya left the pueblo. But their spirits remained in the kiva for four days, where the people cared for them and fed them.

Everything went well. During that winter there was plenty of game. Their weapons weren't strong at this time. So the snow helped the hunters to catch the animals.

65.

*The two societies of Katsina impersonators start
to initiate new members. The medicine men bring
life to the new Katsina masks.*

A long time passed. More and more members were added to
the Katsina and Kopishtaiya societies. Antelope Man gave
them authority to initiate new members. They could do this
because, like the medicine men, they were agents of supernatural authority.

Antelope Man called in different men at different times
and revealed secretly what to do. He talked of everything
that had happened, how the people had done wrong, and
how they were now imitating the real Katsinas who could no
longer come in person. He advised the initiates not to take
this lightly, not to mock, but to believe. The men who impersonated the Katsinas had the power and right to kill any who
joked about them. He said they should not tell anyone who
was not initiated that so-and-so was a Katsina. This way
many men came and asked to become members.

More time passed. Many children grew up. Those who
wished were brought into the kiva to learn from those who
were already members. The newcomers were taught about
making masks, prayer sticks, songs, and prayers. Usually
relatives instructed their own relatives.

Country Chief took sacred corn meal, selected a society
member, and then brought in one or two boys. "I've brought
you a son [or sons] [saying their names and clans]," he told the
member. "You'll be their father. You'll teach them the secrets
of your society. Help them make their masks and see that they
make no serious mistakes."

As was done before, Country Chief asked the medicine
men to give life to these masks. Everything followed the same

course except that new members were initiated out in the countryside. There the initiator hit them hard, four times on their backs. After the new member was struck he was supposed to yell like a Katsina. In this way he became a member for life.

66.

The Country Chief creates a sacred clown society. The painting, adornment, and fetishes of this Ko-shari Society are taught. When they enter the pueblo, the Koshari make jokes and do things backward and serve as communicators between the Katsinas and the people.

When Country Chief saw how much work there was to distribute the gifts he thought of calling on the Koshari. So he asked two medicine men to represent them. Giving them tobacco and corn meal, he said, "You're to give cigarettes to whomever you wish to be Koshari." Going from man to man they asked, "Maybe you'd like a smoke?" But instead of handing a smoke to the man who accepted, they trapped him. Two men were caught this way, and the medicine men notified Country Chief that they would be initiated.

When Country Chief was ready he had the medicine men bring them in. They told the initiates how to represent Koshari. They tried to back out but were told, "You've been caught by the sacred tobacco. Unless you go on with this you'll be haunted by the Koshari whose spirit was in the smoke." So they thought it best to go on with it.

The next day the Katsinas were supposed to arrive. Again the initiates were brought before Country Chief. Before they entered the kiva he had them come down the ladder the wrong way, head first. They acted as best they could.

Country Chief prepared medicine before them. He'd already worked on their songs and prayers. First they took off their clothes. Then he sang. Whenever a certain place in the song was reached, some medicine was sprinkled over them.

He painted their faces with white clay, drawing black circles around their eyes and mouths and black horizontal stripes on their bodies. Their hair was tied standing up in two bunches, just like the real Koshari. These represented clouds.

The medicine men had skinned two small canyon wrens but left their hearts inside. These had been dried and were fetishes. They also prepared two mockingbirds to hang down as necklaces. These gave the Koshari the power to talk fast and chatter and mimic. In this way they were initiated.

They were to be in charge of the Koshari. Each would initiate his eldest son and anyone else who wished to become a member. The medicine men said they were to represent the real Koshari, who had the habit and right of going wherever they pleased, even to the most sacred places.

The medicine men said they would not know sadness. Even if they were injured they would not feel pain. Nor would they get sick. "You'll also have the power of a medicine man," they said. "If one of them makes medicine you can go in and take it without permission and leave and cure anyone you wish."

They made one Honani for both of them and gave it to the first initiated, as he was to be the Koshari leader. Later all Koshari could use it. This ceremony took all night.

By morning Messenger Katsina was announcing in the plaza that the Koshari were coming. Upon hearing this they rushed out, climbed on the rooftops, and began yelling. Leaping down the Koshari ran up to Messenger Katsina. "Maybe you want something here?" they asked. "I want Antelope Man and Country Chief," he replied. "Well, we'll get them," they said.

The Koshari found Antelope Man and Country Chief and said they were wanted in the plaza. While they met with Messenger Katsina and continued their ritual, the Koshari stood around making jokes. As was custom, Country Chief relayed the message brought by Messenger Katsina, declaring it in the streets. Behind him came the Koshari, mocking his movements, twisting his statements and reversing their meanings.

As the entire body of Katsinas arrived the Koshari ran ahead of everyone else to greet them. Were they the Katsinas, they wanted to know. When they said, "Yes," the Koshari began sprinkling corn meal and leading them through the pueblo. Everything followed in the usual way, except there was a larger group of dancers.

Now the Koshari acted as interpreters between the Katsinas and the people. Since the Katsinas never speak, they used sign language, which the Koshari understood. The Koshari took the presents brought by the Katsinas and distributed them so the people could not observe the Katsinas too closely.

All day they danced. Towards the last of the dances the Katsinas were about to throw more gifts. Noticing the people crowding too near the Katsinas, the Koshari thought of making a boundary line of ashes. This was their trap, they said. If anyone crossed the line they would make him a Koshari. In this way everyone was kept back. After each dance they were careful to destroy the line.

All went well. The sun was setting and the customary ceremony of praying took place. The Katsinas departed. The dancers went out to the hiding place and unmasked with the same ceremonies as before and returned their masks to the kiva.

This is how the Katsinas are still represented in the pueblo.

67.

A new disease arrives. The Twins save the people, then search for victims among other peoples. The council decides it is time to leave White House. The people move towards the place known as Ha'ako.

For a long time life went on this way and all was well.

Then a sickness fell upon the people at White House. It was a disease with blisters all over the body. Death came to many for the first time. The population decreased rapidly.

The medicine men did their best, but it was too much for them. The people grew unhappy. They were dying too fast to go through the proper ceremonies. When someone passed away they just wrapped him up and the family buried him.

The only ones who did not get sick were the Twins. Probably this was because of their father's power. When they tried to cure the sickness with this power it didn't always work. So they tried harder and each time they saved some of their people and managed to check the disease.

By now the Twins had traveled around a lot and knew other people. So they thought they'd go out and learn whether they were sick or not. They went northwest and southwest, all around, and found many of them. But none were sick. The Twins were hated by these other people, who didn't know them.

Upon their return they called a meeting of the medicine men, Country Chief, and Antelope Man. "I guess our mother Iatiku doesn't want us to live here anymore," they said. They remembered that she'd told them to go on south to the place known as Ha'ako. "Maybe the sickness is a sign that we should move on." The council decided to do so.

Country Chief told the people they'd leave in four days.

That gave them time to prepare provisions and make new moccasins and take what they needed. He also ordered that nothing belonging to their religion, their altars and masks and other things, must be left behind. All were to assist in carrying them on their journey.

68.

The people travel across four mountains and through four valleys. They create the exorcism ritual to put the sickness behind them. At Sage Basin they rebuild their pueblo and kivas and resume their lives as before.

When the fourth day came Country Chief told the medicine men to go on ahead about four lengths, a long ways, and prepare a place to stop. So they started out. At their first stop they dressed in their official outfits. On the south side of their camp they made a sand painting to represent the four mountains.

When the people followed they were to step across these four mountains and valleys on the ground. In this way they put the sickness that much more behind them. All the people that arrived walked over the painting, stepping on a mountain and valley in turn. As each one approached, the medicine men on the south side brushed off the sickness with their pairs of medicine feathers.

They explained how the people were to stop halfway up the mountain, then stop on top, then stop in the valley, then stop halfway up, and so forth. As they brushed them off with the medicine feathers they said, "Come, Raven! You represent the whirlwind. Sweep away from us this sickness and all diseases and sadness. You're the one with the real power to do this." For each person they repeated this as they stepped up and walked across the sand painting.

At the other end of the painting were two medicine men. Close to the ground, as though they were still growing, they held two yucca plants cut off at the root. When a person came over the fourth mountain he spit his sadness into the middle of the plant.

Two more medicine men stood nearby. Laid out on the ground were four yucca leaves tied together at the corners to form a frame. As each person stepped into it the medicine men swung it four times backward to spill his sickness behind him. After passing through the frame, they were told to continue to a high place where there were still two more medicine men. Before reaching that place they were to pick up any object that caught their eye, any stick or stone, and brush themselves with it, telling it to take away their sickness and sorrow. Then they were allowed to go on.

Everyone went through this. The medicine men buried the objects carrying the disease in a hole that had been dug between them. They finished by destroying the painting of the mountains and banishing the sickness for good. Lastly they did all this to each other. Then they made four marks on the ground with an arrowhead, blocking the trail, as a barrier to the disease.

For a long time they traveled slowly, as they were on foot and heavily burdened. Finally they arrived at a place named Sage Basin. Here the country was beautiful and they found water. "We'll stop here for four years and make a pueblo," Country Chief told the people. "Here we'll take a long rest."

They made houses with stones and settled down. They built their kivas and carried on their ceremonies and lived as before.

69.

On their travels, the Twins discover some Corn clan Katsinas. The people set up a Corn clan altar for them. Those Katsinas visit the pueblo, accompanied by the little fire-carrying Katsina.

While they were living at Sage Basin the Twins traveled all around the country. During their wanderings they found a group of Katsinas belonging to the Corn clan. Each one had a different name. When the Twins returned home they reported that they had found these real Katsinas.

"They belong to us," said members of the Corn clan. "They're our relatives. We'll be their friends." Not knowing how to call these Katsinas, the Corn clan leader asked the medicine men whether he should make an altar for them.

"They're real Katsinas," the medicine men replied. "They must have an altar." He told Corn Man that he would first have to have his own altar, for without it he could not call them.

Instructing him how to make it, he had the Corn clan leader collect oak sprouts that were about a year old. The Twins described how these Katsinas carried canes, so the medicine man told him to bend several of the sprouts into crooks. The medicine man also made four Honani for their altar, but they were to lie flat, as corn cobs are piled on their sides, and not set up on end.

One of the Corn Katsinas always had fire on him. He was small and carried a little canteen which was miraculously kept full of water. So the medicine men thought of calling him to bring some of this water to pour into the jar belonging to Antelope Man. That way the people would never be out of water. They also thought of having him bring some of his fire, so he could light a fire in the center of the plaza. From there the people could light their hearths at home, and they would always have fire.

The Corn clan leader finished his altar and decided to try it out. Asking his clansmen to make prayer sticks he brought them to it. They did as Antelope Man had done before. They went out and buried the prayer sticks and prayed for the Katsinas to come.

The Katsinas received the sticks and prayers. The people had asked for water and fire, and the Katsinas understood. The people knew they could expect these Katsinas on the fourth day.

All the Corn clan made ready. They washed their heads so they'd look clean and neat. During the four days they purified themselves.

From early in the morning the fourth day was hot. The clan leader told his Corn clan to fast all day. A little after sunrise they saw the little Fire Katsina in the distance with smoke around him. As he approached the pueblo he built a series of fires. Three other Katsinas were with him, and one was a *berdache*. They were not lively and poked along and took some time to get near.

When they approached the pueblo the Corn clan went out to meet them. Country Chief and his officers acted as guards, keeping everyone else away. With corn meal they made a path into the plaza. The Corn clan had built a fireplace in the middle. Country Chief had a jar ready for the water.

The Corn clan leader asked the little Katsina to make fire for them so the people would always have it, and to put water in the jar so they would always have that, too. He was skillful at this.

Following the usual ceremony, all the Katsinas danced four times, but slowly and sluggishly. About noon they left, like real Katsinas, back to their homes to the west of Sage Basin. After the Katsinas left, the people gathered the fire.

70.

When the real Katsinas come to visit, they are mocked once again. To avoid the troubles of the past and remind the people what happened before, the Country Chief decides to reenact the terrible battle between humans and the Katsinas. The Katsina impersonators prepare for the coming drama.

For a long time the people lived at Sage Basin. The real Katsinas came and danced for them. But after a time some men began to mock them again. The War Chief learned their names. He remembered how the Katsinas beat and killed the people when this happened before. He thought the best way to punish the mockers was to dramatize that fight.

So Country Chief called a council of all the people who knew about the Katsinas—Antelope Man and the medicine men. He declared they would do this even if it took the lives of relatives or friends. It was a while before he won their consent, as they knew some of the mockers. Even if someone had a son who had disrespected the Katsinas, he had to help.

They called council after council and picked out the ones to represent two Messenger Katsinas as well as Katsina Chief. Every Antelope clan member, even women and children, were given long staffs to guard against the Katsina impersonators attacking the people. Everyone knew that the Katsinas considered these Antelope clan members as their fathers. If they held a staff out horizontally in front of a Katsina, he would not run against it or overcome them.

Antelope Man also made a wall of stiff buffalo hides which was propped up by three sticks. This represented the pueblo. It was understood that when the Katsina impersonators struck this wall with clubs and weapons they were symbolically whipping the people. They were not really striking them. The wall was set up outside the pueblo, where the Katsinas appeared.

They were careful not to tell those who'd mocked the Katsinas of these plans, as they were to be killed for real.

At this time the Corn clan called its members to make plans in the kiva. They were to carry the hide wall, erect it, and hold it. The men impersonating the Katsinas killed some deer and brought their blood into the kiva. Filling deer intestines with it they distributed them among their members, for wearing around their necks.

The hide wall faced west, with the drama taking place in front of it. Members of the Antelope clan were to stand on each side, winging out from it. The Twins were asked to position themselves at either end. When a Katsina tried to hit them, one twin was to knock him down and cut the blood-filled intestine.

Just before the Katsinas arrived, Antelope Man was to ask the guilty ones to pray with him in the plaza. There the Katsinas would spring out, chasing them around the plaza, catching them, and clubbing them to death. At this point the Twins were to enter the plaza and knock down the Katsinas and pretend to cut their throats.

The Katsina Society members to take part went into the mountains. They cut branches from a hardy oak tree, made tea from them, and purified themselves for four days. On the night of the third day, they carved prayer sticks of hardwood.

71.

*Before the mock battle the Katsina impersonators
gather outside the pueblo. Messenger Katsinas visit
the people and escape as he did in reality before.
The impersonators prepare their attack.*

It was understood that as the Katsinas entered the village
they were to act enraged and fight among themselves. If anyone fell or was killed in this fighting they were not to be
brought into the pueblo. Instead they would be buried in the
wilderness with their masks still on.

When the time came, the impersonators who regarded themselves as manly got together in the kiva. They were not to put
on their full attire or make themselves look attractive. They
painted white all over their bodies. Early the next morning
they went into the country and hid together about four or five
miles from the pueblo.

Meanwhile everyone got ready. They made prayer sticks
and the men and women of the Antelope clan painted up with
pink color all over except for their faces. They put feather
down on their heads. Out came the hide wall. Each woman of
the Antelope clan was given a staff. Masewi, the elder twin,
blessed the wall to lend it power. When the time came they
also called out the Katsina Chief of the Corn clan.

About noon two Messenger Katsinas arrived from Wenimats. They informed Country Chief that the rest of the Katsinas were on their way. The people should bring them presents
for they would be there shortly.

Antelope Man got all the mockers and gathered them at
his altar. He showed them how to make prayer sticks with
which to pray to the Katsinas. He had them wait there.
When the Katsinas arrived he would lead them out.

The Messenger Katsinas refused the offerings of Country
Chief—no tobacco, corn meal or other food. They behaved

just like the real Messenger Katsinas. They carried bows and arrows for which Country Chief first asked, as a gift. But then Antelope Chief and the people forcibly held them and disarmed them.

The Messenger Katsinas ran back to the men who were about to impersonate the Katsinas. They related what just happened, but they exaggerated it. They said they were almost killed. They told them to fight as hard as they could and kill as many as possible.

The men put on their masks and started out. There were many of them. On their way they picked up sticks and tore off strong branches to serve as clubs. Meanwhile the man acting as Katsina Chief was trying to hold them back.

72.

*The Katsina impersonators strike the wall of buf-
falo hides that represents the pueblo. Although
the mockers offer prayer sticks of remorse and
forgiveness, some of them are actually killed. Yet
the War Twins still defeat the invading Katsinas.
The impersonators pretend to die and then pretend to return to life.*

The village prepared for the mock battle. The wall of buffalo hides was in place. The men, women, and children of
the Antelope clan stood in front of it, holding their staffs to
guard the village.

Ahead of the rest, Katsina Chief was first to reach the hide
wall. He leaned against it and rubbed his back against it to
gain strength and courage. When he broke through the wall,
the men fell back into the lines of women. Then the other
Katsinas rushed up and struck the wall four times before
turning around and running away. Now anyone could come
and strike the wall. They all raced to see who was first.

The Antelope clan watched to see that no one struck it
more than four times. The Katsinas tried to pass through,
but clan members held out their staffs and barred the way.
As the rest of the Katsinas approached, the little Fire Katsina was behind the hide wall. He had been dancing since it
was set up, and continued as the Katsinas were striking it.
This left only the Twins to protect the "pueblo."

After all the Katsinas struck the hide wall four times the
little Fire Katsina and the Twins took it down. The line of people closed the gap that was left. The Katsinas were held back
by the Antelope clan. Carrying the hides into the plaza, Katsina Chief and the Twins reerected the wall on the north side.

The mockers were brought from the altar to this place,
unaware that they were about to die. They thought they

were coming to pray to the Katsinas and would be forgiven. But the Katsinas knew what they were going to do.

The Antelope clan women formed wings on either side of the wall. When Antelope Man gave a shout the men holding the Katsinas back turned and ran to the plaza and took their places alongside the women. As the Katsinas rushed in the mockers waited before the wall with their prayer sticks. The Katsinas clubbed them to death.

Now was the turn for the Twins. They caught the two Messenger Katsinas, the leaders in the killing, and castrated them. Bladders filled with deer blood were in their crotches. But Tsitsanits was stationed well back of the wall and the Twins could not reach him. Then the Twins attacked the Katsinas and cut their throats. Their heads sank down and they fell to earth, soaked with deer blood and simulating death. While lying on the ground they prayed that the blood would give new strength to the earth, that the earth would yield more crops.

After Masewi and Oyoyewi killed all the Katsinas they took out their staffs and arrowheads, the medicines their Sun father had given them. Returning to the Katsinas lying on the ground, they brought them back to life. Antelope Man had prayer sticks with him, to use after the Katsinas came alive again. Now they prayed that the real Katsinas would not come back to kill the people.

The Katsina impersonators acted as if they were really brought back to life. This was their dramatization, but the guilty ones, the mockers, were really killed, probably eight or ten of them. After the Antelope men made their prayers, the Katsinas got up and carried the dead out of the village and buried them in the desert.

All this was done to make the people believe more strictly in the Katsinas. The Antelope people took down the wall and stored the pieces away. The little Fire Katsina, who was still dancing all this time, was dismissed and left.

This is how they passed their time at Sage Basin.

73·

Time passes. Angry relatives of the dead mockers move away from the pueblo. Country Chief leads the rest of the people to Tule Lake. There they destroy some ant hills and become sick. The first Ant Society medicine man cures everyone.

A long time went by. Then trouble began again. Some people did not approve of the dramatization, and quarrels started. Some relatives of those killed left the tribe. Others said they were not happy at this place. They decided to leave for the south, remembering that they were to search for Ha'ako in that direction.

Country Chief notified everyone that they were to move. The people were told to take their masks and altars and leave nothing sacred behind. They left with the same ceremonies as before, heading south.

It is not known how far they went. Finally they stopped at a place where they went through the ceremony of forgetting once again. It is not known when they symbolically crossed the four mountains and left their sickness and troubles behind.

They traveled for many moons and came to a place called Tule Lake. The people were tired and asked if they could stop and build another village. So they made camp. They built better and better houses and did not move on.

Here they lived happily for a long time. They forgot their quarrels and troubles. They practiced their ceremonies and enjoyed a full village life as before. Other societies of medicine men were introduced, two or three more altars of the Fire medicine men, three of the Flint medicine men, and three or four more of the Giant medicine men.

At Tule Lake the people found many ant hills. When they constructed their houses they destroyed a number of their homes. People did not think much of ants. They stepped on them and killed them. But there came a time when the people became sick with an unknown disease that caused sores all over their bodies. It seemed as if the ants were always running to those sores as they do to their homes.

The medicine men did all they could, but they failed. In the villages which they left behind or passed by the people had different clan names. One was named the Ant clan and the medicine men decided to create another society from them. They chose a man to be the first Ant Society medicine man and gave him an altar. He would have the power to cure the disease brought on by ants. But he had to learn their prayers and how to move the ants from one place to another so they would not be harmed.

This Ant altar was small and had no prayer sticks. There was one Honani and two eagle wing feathers, the longest feathers, and two hands of a horned toad. This was because the toad eats ants. A patient was painted in red and sat on top of the ground painting. The medicine man swept off the disease with a grass brush. Whatever was brushed off them was gathered in a corn husk and buried.

Nowadays when a house is being built a medicine man is called to remove the ants. He takes some and the owner digs out the rest. In the tradition it was not necessary for the first Ant medicine man to do more than brush each patient once to effect the cure. Everyone got well again.

74·

At Tule Lake the famine and drought return. To bring back the rain the people need a Fire altar. Searching for one in Katsina country, the Twins steal their weather medicine. The Katsinas retaliate with rain and lightning storms that drive the animals and people up a big mountain. The Twins shoot arrows at the rising waters until they subside.

In the original war with the Katsinas the first medicine man, from the Fire Society, was killed. His altar seemed lost with him, for he'd plastered it in a wall to hide it. But when they moved his wife found it and brought it along, although the people didn't know this. In the meantime duplicate altars were made at Tule Lake.

While they were at Tule Lake there came a famine. The people were starving and there was no rain. Through the other medicine men Country Chief and Antelope Man tried to bring rain, but they failed. So they called a meeting and Country Chief asked if anyone knew where the first altar was. The medicine men remembered that it disappeared during the Katsina attack and thought they'd stolen it. The Twins were at this meeting, and Country Chief asked for their help. "Yes," they said, "we'll get it back."

They went home and put on their magical clothes. They were gone for many days. First they went to Wenimats, then to the mountains of the cardinal directions. They entered the sacred places and stirred things up.

They asked the Katsinas if they'd stolen the altar. They said no, but the Twins rudely went on searching. In the meantime the woman who'd kept the altar brought it to Country Chief and asked, "Is this what you've lost?"

But the Twins had angered the Katsinas again. So they called their fellow Katsinas from all the directions, including the rain-makers, to meet at North Mountain to discuss what to do about the Twins. They had behaved badly, but they were still powerful. The council lasted so many days that the Katsinas grew tired.

When the Twins arrived they found them all asleep. The spirit of the North Mountain had his staff for making snow. On the west was the spirit with the staff to make hail. On the south the one with the staff that caused lightning and balls for making thunder. The Twins stole them all. In the east was the spirit with the staff that created frost, and they took that, too.

Meanwhile the people had erected the missing Fire altar. Addressing its Honani as though it were Iatiku herself, the Fire Society medicine man said, "You've promised us a happy life. But we're in need of water. See if you can give us all the water that you have." That was when the medicine man made a mistake. The people did not know why he asked for so much water.

After the Twins stole those staffs they told the Katsinas, "Go on sleeping. We've everything we need. We can use them as well as you can. We'll plant them and challenge you to dig them up. If you can do that, we'll believe in you." This was also a mistake. It made the Katsinas angry.

On their way home the Twins buried the staffs, but not very deeply. When the Katsinas woke up and heard what was said they could do nothing, as the Twins had run off. They held another meeting but were at a loss as to how to beat the Twins.

So they thought of bringing Water Snake to life, which got its name because it travels like a stream of water. They told it to chase the Twins and devour them. "We'll get the staffs back," they said.

The Twins didn't get far from where they'd buried the staffs before a large cloud appeared, then a cloudburst. Lightning struck at them, but they shielded themselves with the buckskin shirts their father had given them. Flints from the lightning got tangled in the leather. The Twins jerked the flints through the shirts and breathed power from them, each saying, "Thank you! With this I'll be more manly."

As they traveled back it rained the whole way. By the time they reached home they found the lake had overflowed and driven out the people. Many were struck by lightning and killed. After the Twins stretched out their buckskins to shield them, no more were hit.

"We give up," said the spirit rulers of the four directions. "I guess we can't kill them." But they let Water Snake follow their instructions.

It continued to rain. The people were driven out of their homes. Taking only their altars and what they needed most they headed south to a high mountain. The medicine men worked at their altars. Country Chief and Antelope Man prayed for the rain to stop. No one listened. Many animals came to this mountain for safety as well as many different peoples. Some spoke different languages, others spoke similarly. All were shielded under the buckskin.

The world began filling with water. Waves almost swept everyone from the mountain. Seeing all this the Twins said, "That must be Water Snake. He's coming to kill us." So far they hadn't used the four arrows from their father. "Perhaps this is where we should use them," they said.

They watched until the biggest wave rose up. "This is where his heart is," they said. Each shot an arrow into it. Then the waves slowed down. They became a huge snake which wrapped itself around the mountain. There the Twins killed it, using the rest of their arrows, each shooting four times.

Everything calmed down and the rain stopped. The water started to lower, but slowly. It is said that formerly the mountains were beautifully smooth and rounded. This flood and the receding waters cut canyons and gullies and made them rough.

It is not known how long they camped on this mountain. But they always had food, and the animals that were saved increased. When things began to dry out the people separated again, not being able to understand each other.

75.

Still carrying the two remaining eggs from Iatiku's basket, the people travel farther south. At the place called Hardwood Pass, they establish a new village and protect it with an altar. They perform a new Katsina dance and conduct ceremonies to produce a successful harvest.

The people were still looking for Ha'ako.

They had not lost the two eggs that Iatiku had given them. "This cannot be the right place," they said. "Our bad luck shows that." They got onto the plains again and moved south. They passed many ruins where people had lived before, and the paths of other people. These peoples were enemies of each other. It is not known how they were saved from the flood.

When attacked by their enemies, the Twins went out alone to fight. Because of their father's power they always won. They thought they would keep track of how many they killed. So after killing an enemy they put their thumb on the head and cut around it to take the scalp.

The people traveled on and passed a place called Lake, where Laguna Pueblo now stands. Here they stopped for the ceremony of forgetting. No town was there at that time. South of the lake they symbolically crossed the four mountains.

When they got to the place they called Antelope Range they asked if they could rest, as they noticed a lot of game. They camped at a big white sandstone rock about ten miles northeast of today's Acoma. On the north side is a place called Turquoise Cave with water coming out. While they camped here they had good luck killing antelope.

Traveling around the region they found the place called Hardwood Pass. The people thought of moving there to build another village. Some said it must be the place called Ha'ako, since there were turkeys and antelope in plenty. They broke camp and built a new village there.

Again they established their altars and ceremonies and the medicine men cleared the place of disease. They always took a basket of prayer sticks that they buried in the center of the proposed site. Under the basket they put an arrowhead to protect the pueblo.

Some people wanted to live at the base of the mesa. But the Twins said it would be better to live on top where they could look around. That way whenever they left it they could look back and see their home standing out and think of it as a wonderful place. It would also furnish protection.

Others did not agree this was the right place. They broke away from those who went along with the Twins. "We've seen another mesa which is more imposing," they said. "We'll build our home there." This was further south and was called Katsima [Enchanted Mesa]. A few families, very few, went up there. But they ran out of water and after a time rejoined those at the other village. They built a pretty village on the low mesa. Here they lived contentedly for a long time because there was much game, including many turkeys. They held ceremonies every season and got along well.

Then came time for planting. Antelope Man recalled that Iatiku had told him that the people should always hold a dance beforehand. So he had Country Chief have them wait to plant. This dance would help all kinds of crops. The people were told to meet in the kiva where Antelope Man would show them how to dance and why.

They were to make images of corn, pumpkins, and beans, as Iatiku had advised, and bring them on the night they met for the dance. They had already learned the songs and dances from her at Shipapu, but they had forgotten most of them.

In the kiva Antelope Man set up his altar. The people came with their images and placed them before it. They recalled some songs and danced all night. In the kiva the men danced for a while in a circle, then they rested and the women danced. This continued until just before sunrise.

Antelope Man had them come up to the altar and retrieve their images. Now they accompanied the prayers and dances. They were to take them and pray in the directions, then plant them in their gardens. This was done and they had abundant harvests.

76.

The Twins gamble with a guard of South Mountain and win. They learn the location of the large rock called Ha'ako. Country Chief and his medicine men invite the Twins to join the search for their future home.

The Twins were helpful to the people, always getting up early to go out into the country to yell at the rain clouds—the Katsinas. It is not known how long they lived at this place.

They were always traveling. One time they went to South Mountain, the home of the summer ruler and the spirit of that direction. When they arrived he had a guard who refused to let anyone in. They asked who he was and he gave a name which meant someone who was a busybody, who always wanted to do something.

They discovered he was a good gambler, quick-witted and a strong kick stick runner. He challenged the Twins to different games. He taught them a new game, how to win arrows from each other. They put up a target and whoever got closest to it won. This guard knew they had the sacred arrows and wanted them.

So they held a race on which they bet the arrows. But the guard was old and got lost, so the Twins won everything he put up. He became angry. He still had the baby's head made up to look like a ball and filled with blood. But the Twins did not want to gamble for this just yet. First they wanted the spirit of the South to tell them where Ha'ako was. Since they had not seen him so far they asked his guard.

"Maybe you know the place called Katsima," he replied. "Ha'ako is just southwest of that place—a large rock. You'll find it by going to the northeast and yelling. When you hear the echo very distinctly, that's where you're looking for."

In exchange for this information he wanted the Twins to

return their winnings, but they refused. "You started the betting and taught us to gamble," they said. "You lost, your properties are ours." Again the guard asked, but again the Twins said no. A third time he asked, and a fourth. Still they refused.

Then the old man hit his ball with a stick. Blood splattered against the wall of the house. When it fell to the floor it cried like a baby. The Twins got frightened and ran off with their winnings. The old man chased them, hitting the ball towards them, which kept wailing like a child. Item by item, the Twins dropped everything they had won. After escaping from the guard at last, they stopped and talked it over. "This is the first time I've ever been frightened," said one. "Were you frightened, too? He must have supernatural power." They thought no more about it and returned home.

There they stayed a long time. One day they went to Country Chief and told him that the real Ha'ako was that place further south, and left the rest to him. He was the one to look for it and see if the echo was there.

Country Chief called the medicine men to a meeting and gave them the information which Masewi and Oyoyewi brought from South Mountain. He said that he still had the two eggs that Iatiku had given them to bring to Ha'ako. "We shouldn't stay here any longer," Country Chief said. "I'll go ahead and find out if it is the right place." They set a date to leave with some of the medicine men and invited the Twins along.

So they went to the south to look for Ha'ako.

77·

They find the rock where they should live and Country Chief prepares the people for the move. First he makes them choose between the differently colored eggs to decide who will remain at Ha'ako. While the parrot group leaves for the south, the crow group builds a pueblo at the foot of the rock.

They saw the rock and went towards the northeast end. When Country Chief cried out, "Ha'ako," they all listened. Four times he yelled to make sure. Every time the echo came back clearly. All agreed that this must be the place.

Returning to the people they met again. They remembered that they were instructed to break the parrot egg at Ha'ako, but to take the crow's egg on afterwards to Kuyapukauwak. They decided to move, as the distance was far and they had been told by Iatiku to go there.

Country Chief gave the people four days to prepare. They were to leave nothing behind. The people were glad they were close to Ha'ako and anxious to move.

On the fourth day they left, and that day reached the foot of the rock. They gathered close around Country Chief. He held up the two eggs. "These were given us by Iatiku," he said. "One is a parrot egg, the other a crow egg. You're to choose the egg you think is the parrot one."

One at a time he had them step up. Placing the two eggs on a piece of buckskin, he told each father or head of family to stand on the side they thought was the one with the parrot egg. First the medicine men made their choice, then the rest. After this came one woman about to bear a child. "When my baby comes," she said, "she'll belong to the Parrot clan."

Country Chief picked up the egg chosen by the Twins. "This will be the parrot egg," he said. "Those who've chosen this egg will live here, at Ha'ako." He told the people that they could not take back their choice, but must remain on the side they had selected. The parrot was supposed to be a pretty bird and would be useful, he said. But the crow would be a pest and good for nothing.

Most of the medicine men and Country Chief himself were on the side of the egg he was about to break. First he stepped back, telling everyone to watch carefully. This egg was blue and pretty, while the other was a dull color.

He started to count—one, two, three, four. On the fourth count he threw the blue egg against the rock. When it broke a number of crows flew out. The losers felt bad. But they couldn't retract, because Iatiku had told them if they did so they'd never live happily anywhere. Country Chief said, "This ends our journey. The rest must travel on to Kuyapu-kauwak and take the other egg with them."

Everyone camped together at this place. Some medicine men joined those who were to continue south. They were given their altars and some masks. But since most of the officials remained, they made new ones for the departing group. To create a new Country Chief the old Country Chief chose someone and instructed him in his duties. He was provided with duplicates of the necessary things. Antelope Man did the same, appointing a man to take his place with the other group.

When the time finally came to separate they drew together. Country Chief and Antelope Man told those who were leaving who their officers were to be. It was a sad moment for everyone. Then the parrot group left towards the south. It is not known how far they went.

Those who remained were told by Country Chief to build a village at the foot of this rock, and so they did. It is not known how long they lived here. They carried on their ceremonies as before. They were lucky and happy because they had come to their final home.

78.

The gods of the four directions agree to punish the Twins for their misdeeds. They send an evil spirit in the guise of a beautiful woman to sleep with them. But she transforms into an evil hag and haunts them. The Twins run for help, but no one comes. The guardian of the South chases the evil spirit away with his bloody game ball.

As usual Masewi and Oyoyewi were busy traveling in different countries, killing many and bringing back scalps. The rulers in the four directions did not like the Twins. So they held a meeting and decided that they were behaving too badly. They seemed afraid of nothing and nobody. The rulers decided they must be punished.

They called an old man, an evil spirit, to help them. When he arrived they described all the wrongs the Twins were doing and asked him to do it. "Yes, I'm glad to help," he said. "Leave it to me. I'll find a way."

This evil spirit watched the village at Ha'ako for someone to die. The Twins knew a girl of good character. The spirit worked on her and caused her to die. At the time of her death, he entered her house, painted himself with some of her blood, and assumed her likeness.

Meeting the Twins he spoke to them. This girl was attractive. The Twins liked her and invited her home. She told them she loved them and wanted to live with them. They told their mother what she wanted, and she was pleased. They let her stay overnight. While the Twins slept she crept between them, but they did not know it.

While Masewi and Oyoyewi were sleeping the girl turned into a corpse with a horrible appearance. When she fondled one of them he woke up. She looked like an old hag. He cried out, "Look, someone has lain down with us." Before his brother could answer, the girl tried to pull them back. "It's me," she said. "You're my husband. Don't you remember inviting me to live here?" The Twins were so frightened that they ran out with the evil spirit close behind. This spirit was called Ko'ko—she was also known as a haunt. (And so, if a man murders another, he is always haunted by a Ko'ko in the night.)

All night she pursued them. The Twins ran some distance and tried to rest, but she caught up and spoke to them. In this manner she kept after them for days and nights. Running to North Mountain they entered the home of the northern ruler and requested his help. "Yes," he said, "I'll help you." At last they got some rest.

Then the evil spirit drew closer. "Are my husbands in here?" she yelled. The northern ruler was aware this evil spirit was out to punish them. "Yes, they're here," he answered. "Come down and get them." The evil spirit entered and again asked the Twins why they were running away and tried to coax them back.

They fled with the evil spirit at their heels. Every time they tried to rest, it woke them up. They ran and ran until they arrived at Wenimats and entered Tsitsanits' kiva, begging for help. He, too, knew they were being punished, but he let them stay. Yet when the evil spirit arrived, Tsitsanits let her in. He warned the Twins they should leave because he could only provide temporary shelter. Once more they ran with the spirit pursuing them.

On they raced to West Mountain. They had not eaten since leaving home and were hungry and tired. When they asked the ruler of the west for help he agreed but wanted to know what was wrong with the bows and arrows they had used for killing people. They said they were too scared to shoot straight. The western ruler promised to help. Yet he, too, knew they must be punished, and allowed the spirit in. "Take your husbands," he told her. "You're so ugly I can't do anything with you."

Again the Twins took off, this time heading for the gambler of South Mountain. By now they were exhausted. The spirit was gaining on them and they were ready to give up. Rushing into the gambler's house they frightened him. They said he had nothing to fear, they were being chased and this was their last hope. The gambler was flattered that two such brave men should plead for his assistance. "Yes, I'll help you. You can rest here," he said. "What's wrong, you're not so manly anymore?"

He took his stick and the ball made of the baby's head. When the evil spirit yelled for the Twins, the gambler answered, "Yes, they're here, come in." Then he hit the ball, it struck her chest, blood splashed, and the ball cried out. The spirit was so terrified she turned around and fled.

Following with his stick, the gambler continued striking the ball. He was a good runner and hit the spirit four times. On the fourth strike the ball chased her back into its home. Then he came back and let the ball chase the spirit on its own.

79.

The guardian of South Mountain scolds the Twins for killing people on their travels. He has them create a ceremony to care for scalps and purify themselves. The Twins are subdued when they return home and announce the upcoming scalp ceremony.

By now the Twins were almost dead from exhaustion. The gambler of South Mountain came back and laughed at them. "It's not true after all that you're so brave," he said. "I've won that title from you. Let me tell you why you've been punished. You've been killing people all over the country and leaving their bodies scattered everywhere. That's why this evil spirit was chasing you."

"From now on," he said, "don't kill just for sport or just because you think you're so brave. Human beings are precious. They're not like animals. I guess you know how many scalps you've taken. I'm going to send you back to your people. When you get there take your scalps and wash them. You must also dance for the public. Starting with the day you wash them you will fast for thirty days and observe continence. After the thirtieth day you will come out and dance."

The Twins were told to call the Koshari impersonators to take the lead. The gambler taught them how to perform it and handle the scalps. They were to carry cedar branches, one scalp hanging from each twig. Four days before the dance they should erect them in the plaza. On the fourth day they would come out and dance. After finishing at sundown they could take them down. For thirty more days they were to remain continent.

He warned them, "If you don't keep this fast the evil spirit will come and haunt you again." The scalps were to be preserved, since after the dance they belonged to the entire tribe. With these instructions the Twins went home.

When they reached the village they seemed sad and run down. Country Chief asked what was wrong. "Yes, I guess we do look like that," they said. "We won't tell you now, wait until tonight. Call the people to a meeting. Have the medicine men and officers present."

So Country Chief went up the streets announcing it. In the evening at the appointed time everyone convened in the kiva. Country Chief collected the Twins. When they arrived they weren't smiling and didn't appear as happy or alert and lively as usual. They seemed to have lost their aggressiveness. Whispers were going around. "Why do they look like this? Someone must have beaten them."

Country Chief gave the Twins cigarettes as an offering to rest and smoke before explaining why they'd called the meeting. After he smoked, Masewi, the elder, rose. "Yes, it's true," he said, "I know you're talking about us. We made a mistake. You've always known us to act superior. We never told you, but we killed many people in our travels and left their bodies scattered all around.

"For this reason we were punished by the rulers of the directions, the Katsinas, and others. The evil spirit was brought to life and sent against us. That almost got the best of us. But the gambler of South Mountain helped us beat it. For eight days and nights we were without sleep or food or water. But we survived and have brought instructions from the ruler of that mountain which must be followed from now on.

"We must dance with the scalps of those we killed. First we'll set a date to purify ourselves and confess to Iatiku, with prayers, whose people we've destroyed. We tell you this so you can witness how we go through this ceremony. Watch and listen and learn every step. We also request Country Chief to ask the Koshari to join this ceremony, which they will conduct afterwards. This is why we wanted this meeting. I hope we've not caused too much trouble. You will hear the date for this ceremony when we set it."

The people talked among themselves and agreed the Twins had been too impetuous and forward.

80.

In their ceremony, the Twins are assisted by their mother, the people, and the ants. They stage a mock attack on the scalps and bring them home as trophies so as to honor their warriors.

Upon returning home the Twins told their mother she was to act womanly and help them with what they had to undergo. Offering a prayer to her they said she had a part to play. They knew hers would be the most difficult, for she had to dance all day long. The next day they would start their fast.

Although they were still sick and tired they went and got twigs for prayer sticks. For four days they worked on them, putting them in baskets until four were filled. They also made new outfits. They strung bear claws for a necklace, sewed clothing from the skins of game animals and a shoulder bandoleer from skins of prey animals. To this they attached a pouch which held gravel from ant hills. The flint arrowheads which they had pulled through the skin when lightning chased them at Tule Lake were sewn to the inside as well. Tassels hanging from the pouch were cut from different kinds of skins. All parts of it were taken from enemies they had killed.

After the twelfth day they called Country Chief to instruct his people to compose songs to be used in dramatizing the bringing of scalps into the pueblo. He did as requested. One song was for when the scalps were brought in. They were to sing all night until the sun rose.

On the eighth day, at midnight, Masewi and Oyoyewi took the scalps and walked a ways into the country. Stopping at an ant hill, they broke it up and put the scalps on it. Over the scalps they made a miniature house. They asked the ants to "whip" and "kill" and "eat" the scalps. And the ants did so.

Jumping back and forth over the pile the Twins uttered their war cry. They had brought one basket filled with prayer sticks and prayed with them to the north direction. They buried these sticks and left the scalps.

The next night they went to the west with another basket of prayer sticks, then returned and rested. The following night they went to the south and did likewise, and on the fourth night to the east and did the same. But the fourth time they did not return and continued on to where they'd left the scalps.

Already they had Country Chief announce their arrival with their war cry. When they did so everyone heard them. He called for all the able-bodied men to enter the plaza. Still giving their war cries, Masewi and Oyoyewi drew near.

But Country Chief made them hurry, because the people were frightened. Stepping into the crowd the Twins said, "The enemies are coming after us. We've killed some of them." They had all healthy men prepare their weapons and bring a little lunch. Most rushed home to get them. This was the first time they ever went on a warpath, and the women encouraged them.

Every man came out, none lagged behind. Masewi and Oyoyewi led the attack. When they arrived at the scalps the Twins said, "Here's the place." All shot arrows and threw clubs at the scalps. After the Twins gave orders to stop they told the men that now they were going to "take a scalp." Up they rushed to the miniature house, acting as though they were fighting and cutting scalps from their enemies. One after another they took the scalps and threw them over their shoulders.

After they gathered them up the Twins told the people to get young cedar shoots and cut a twelve-foot pole. The shoots were tied at its top, from each hung a scalp. After this they said, "We're going to take the scalps back to the village and sing the first song."

Approaching the village they sang about twenty songs. Masewi carried the pole. No one else could touch it. If anyone did so he would be haunted by the same evil spirit who had chased the Twins.

The women gathered around them. The pole was planted

in the middle of the plaza. Masewi said, "Four days from now my brother and I will dance. But I ask all of you to help us. During these four days you'll practice this dance. Our mother will do her part."

He told them, "This is the way you are to pay tribute to your warriors if they conquer other people."

81.

For the rest of the scalp ceremony the Koshari take over. During the next four days they rule the pueblo. After this the Twins behave themselves, but they are unhappy. With their mother they finally disappear into the top of the rock at Ha'ako.

That night Country Chief asked the Koshari to come out of the kiva. Going from house to house they collected people to practice in the kiva. During those four days Masewi told them to look upon the Koshari as their rulers, ranking even above Country Chief, Antelope Man, and the medicine men. No one could have cigarettes unless they asked the Koshari for them.

Each sundown the Koshari gathered them in the kiva. The Twins helped with the songs, encouraged everyone to be brave and patient, and fixed their dance attire. They asked two medicine men to dress them. They were still supposed to be resting and not helping themselves, so they instructed the medicine men how to paint and outfit them. This would be the first time everyone saw the Twins in the dress their father had given them and learned how they were painted.

The last night before the dance they practiced with their mother in the kiva. They made different headdresses for her. Koshari told the people to assemble in the kiva before sunrise. About daybreak the Koshari left the kiva wearing their attire and stood on the housetop and sang a song. They went from house to house calling everyone out.

Once the sun came up the Koshari said the dance should begin. The people took their positions. The mother of the Twins went and danced among the men as they entered the plaza. When the song was finished they stopped and she danced alone, with Masewi and a medicine man sitting before her and the pole behind. After she danced one song, they returned to the kiva to rehearse more. For the first dance Masewi, the elder, came out. For the second, Oyoyewi, the younger, appeared.

The Twins had asked some women to prepare food at their home. Being great hunters, the Twins always had plenty of meat. At noon the Koshari told everyone that the women would bring food. Some ate outside, some in the kiva. The Koshari said that after the meal they would dance through the afternoon until sundown. This was the first time the people ever held a feast all together.

When the dancing was done the Twins offered a prayer for the people and thanked them for taking part. Everyone left and rested. The Twins took down the pole and said now the scalps belonged to the tribe. Anyone wishing to be brave could come and ask the scalps for power. Whenever an enemy was killed they should go through this ceremony. It paid respect to that enemy and made sure he would not haunt the killer.

They removed the scalps from the pole, took them home, and built a special addition for the scalps to live in. For thirty days more they were to purge themselves and remain continent. After that they would be free of the evil spirit. This ended the ceremony.

From that day forward the Twins were more careful and less impetuous and purposeless in their activities. Every time a man killed an enemy, they held this ceremony and the people followed their instructions for how to perform it.

But the Twins were unhappy. They said they were not fit to live with the people and were going to disappear. They announced that they would take their mother and go to the top of the east point of the rock at Ha'ako. They chose this place because they knew that Iatiku meant for the people to live on top of the rock, as it would be more wonderful and mysterious.

"We're going ahead in order to disappear there," they said. Shortly after this Masewi, Oyoyewi, and their mother were missed by the people.

82.

A new Country Chief has the medicine men clear a way up the rock. With prayer sticks the people bless this Rainbow Trail and the future locations of their plaza and kivas. The people build their pueblo and clear the freshwater cisterns and are cleansed of disease. One by one the clans climb up the mesa, and life at Ha'ako begins.

It is not known how long they lived at the bottom of the rock, but much time elapsed. Many officers died away. Finally there came a time when Kasewat was Country Chief, being the only son of the War Chief.

The older people remembered that Masewi decreed that eventually they were to move on top of the rock. In that way they would be protected, for these people were the "chosen people." So they decided to carry out Kasewat's plan.

There were still many pine trees on top of the mesa. The medicine men went ahead and planted their prayer sticks on the site. Country Chief asked the men to go up and clear and level it. He had them make a trail to the top on the south side. It was called the Rainbow Ladder.

The medicine men were asked to bring down all the ants. They also moved down the other living things that were not wanted there, like centipedes and snakes.

Kasewat made a duplicate of his broken prayer stick and buried it where the plaza would be. He asked the medicine men to make four lengths of prayer sticks to create a trail to the center of the plaza. The Antelope clan placed their prayer sticks where their headquarters would be. The rest of the medicine men did likewise, planting their prayer sticks at locations where their kivas would be. Country Chief did the same for the public kivas, and for his headquarters.

When all was ready, Country Chief and the Antelope clan were the first to be assisted in building their houses. Everyone helped.

After finishing one place, Country Chief declared what clan would come next. This way they helped each other.

Before they finished all the buildings, the water ran out. So they cleaned out the hollow places in the rock for cisterns, and walled in some so that they would hold more water. When the next rains came they had plenty.

They built the homes for the Antelope clan. After all the houses were finished Country Chief told the people that it was time to move up onto "the completely kerneled long ear of corn," which meant the rock itself.

So the medicine men were first to go up the Rainbow Trail. Before the people climbed up they brushed disease from them. The medicine men helped the people. First they ascended the mesa, then the rest of the people below asked for permission.

Country Chief came to the bottom of the trail and yelled, "Up on top, Country Chief asks if he will be allowed to come up." The medicine men answered, "Yes, come on up. Bring all your game, all your beads, all your crops. Bring long life and leave nothing behind. Come up."

Along the trail the medicine men made different places where they were to go and pray. One of them went along to instruct the people as they climbed. The first place was where the lion would guard them. Next was where the bear would guard. Then was where the green frog would guard. Near the top was the last, where the snake would guard.

At each of these places Country Chief prayed to the different guardians. Then the medicine men let him pass. He was formally directed to his house.

Then came the Antelope clan. The rest in turn climbed up in the same manner. The medicine men directed all of them to their houses.

It took two days to move all the people up, for every ceremonial detail was observed by each clan and society.

After all the people had moved up the medicine men were asked by Country Chief to initiate the kivas and put guards on each of the four walls.

After all was completed they lived for a long time there. Year after year they continued to go through their ceremonies.

This is as far as the tradition is told.

Glossary

These definitions serve in the place of footnotes. Readers desiring more linguistic information and cultural details should consult Leslie A. White's annotations in this myth's original 1942 edition, from which certain phrases in the following notes are taken, as indicated.

Antelope clan—The leading clan at Acoma, from which the man filling the lifelong post of Cacique, or community religious leader, is chosen.

Antelope Place—Known as *Kutsekatsa*, the location where migrating Acoma people camped after Laguna.

berdache—Men who dress and live as women.

Cacique—A term of Caribbean Arawak Indian origin, meaning "chief" and used by the Spanish to designate native leaders. Known as Tiamunyi at Acoma, this term has become the generic Pueblo term for a key religious leader. Drawn from Antelope clan at Acoma, the cacique's lifelong position is less political than spiritual. The community's most honored and respected individual, he is chief counselor, Sun-Watcher, host and "father" to Katsina visitors, "mother" of the pueblo, and ultimate authority in community matters.

cardinal directions (Sacred Mountains)—As with Pueblo cosmologies in general, Acoma mythology and ritual practice pay special attention to four sacred mountains; in each dwells a resident spirit, or "ruler." Each direction also has its color, seasonal, animal, and vegetal associations.

clan—Social units connecting generations related through the female line at Acoma. They are also exogamous, meaning one should not marry within one's unilineal descent group. White (1932) counted fourteen clans (Eagle, Sun, Bear, etc.) in 1926; today the tribe publicly claims thirteen clans.

corn ear—As the Acoma staff of life, ears of corn are often treated as sacred objects. Adorned with cloth and jewels, they are featured in altars and can become central fetishes in their own right. Their collected pollen and specially ground corn meal are used in various, everyday ritual fashion to bless mealtimes and impending journeys, or anytime that safety and harmony are desirable. They are a central emblem of growth, and also remind people of the primary item in the Pueblo diet.

fetish—Small, carved stone representations of animals, especially those of the "prey" category, such as mountain lions, that are used by hunters in rituals for success in killing the category of "game" animals, such as rabbits and antelope.

Ha'ako—The original name for Acoma Pueblo and mesa. Translated as either "Place of Preparedness," stressing its defensible attributes, or "The Prepared Place," suggesting its predestined role as an already blessed location that awaits the coming of the first Acoma migrants.

Hardwood Gap (or Pass)—Known as *Dyaptsiam*, the village site with abundant turkeys and antelope where Acoma migrants lived before reaching Enchanted Mesa and Ha'ako itself.

Honani—White describes this important priestly emblem as "the cotton-wrapped, bead-and-feather-decked corn ear fetish" used by curing societies. It represents Iatiku, "mother" of Indians. At other Keresan-speaking pueblos, Iatiku told the people to make this fetish before leaving, so her living image would always remain with them.

Iatiku—Also known as "Bringing to Life," "mother of all Indians," and "Corn mother," she is one of the two primordial sisters. While the motif of two cocreators is found throughout North America, this version singles out Iatiku as primogenitor of the Acoma people, while her sister is identified with the origin of non-Indians. She epitomizes the generative principle and is represented as a perfect ear of corn.

Katsima—Meaning "Braced Cliff," but also known as "Enchanted Mesa," the small, sheer sandstone mesa is located a little over two miles northeast of Ha'ako, where some migratory families lived, leaving pottery, stone tools, and ladder holes.

Katsina—Important anthropomorphic spirit beings, variously defined as ancestors, clouds, and rain-makers, who are nourished by aromas of tobacco rather than food. They appear mostly in summertime, in companies or individually. Only initiated males and females partake in Katsina Society ceremonies and impersonate them through the donning of buffalo hide masks that are painted according to their specific characters.

Keresan—The language family spoken with similar dialects by the western Keresan group of pueblos, Acoma and Laguna, with more differentiated dialects found among the five eastern Keresan pueblos located along the Rio Grande River.

kiva—Known as *kaanch* in the Keresan language, at Acoma there are five of these sacred meeting chambers to which individuals belong, plus two additional chambers of all-community importance. Kivas are used for ritual and meditative purposes, and also act as men's workshops for making and storing ritual items and regalia. At Acoma they are rectangular, built into houseblocks, and identified by freshly painted ladders, with some uppermost braces carved in the stepped-pyramid symbol to represent rain clouds. Although the myth describes Iatiku's original kiva as circular, one theory about their present shape is that this was to disguise them and their activities from suppression by the Spanish.

Kopishtaiya—Masked winter supernaturals, appearing at winter solstice, regarded as health- and strength-supplying spirits and associated with male warriors.

Koshari—Also known as *Kacale* at Acoma, these sacred clowns impersonate the original Koshari who dwell with Katsinas at Wenimats. Key functionaries who belong to their own secret society, their bodies are painted in white and black horizontal bands, with black rings around their eyes and mouth. In corn husk headdress, breechcloth, and bare feet, they accompany the dancers, both protecting them from onlookers who get too close and amusing everyone with their bawdy, backward actions and irreverent statements.

Laguna Pueblo—Known as *Kawaika*, or "Lake," formally established in the late seventeenth century on an earlier-occupied site associated with a nearby lake. A stopover for early Acoma migrants, Old Laguna is located forty-two miles west of Albuquerque, and today is New Mexico's second-largest Pueblo Indian reservation.

Masewi—The elder of the War Twins.

medicine society—Known as *Shianyi* at Acoma, secret priesthoods of healers or shamans who are dispersed into "societies" that specialize in ailments they are empowered to cure. Once numerous, at Acoma they were reduced by the early twentieth century to primarily three: the Flint, Fire, and Shiwanna societies. Members are trained in preparing altars, conducting seasonal rites, making and depositing prayer sticks, gaining proficiency in relevant prayers and chants, matching particular health problems with proper herbs and plants, and counteracting witches that cause disease. As the profession demands much from its practitioners, recruitment can involve involuntary situations that make an individual open to initiation (such as Edward Hunt's near-death experience after being kicked into a coma by a horse), or "trapping" of potential members.

Messenger Katsina—The Acoma name is *Gomaiowish*. They are assigned roles as communicators among their fellow Katsinas and Acoma villagers.

Mount Taylor—Known as *Kawetsima*, the sacred mountain of the north whose summit shrine, a natural cavity, is a destination for pilgrimages and periodic deposits of prayer sticks.

Nautsiti—Also known as "More of Everything in the Basket," she is the second of the two primordial sisters. The myth contrasts her as having a lighter complexion, quicker mind, and closer tie to non-Indian goods and foods. At Laguna Pueblo, Christian influence is said to have transformed her into a man, "the father of the Whites."

Nawish—A group of Katsinas known as farmers. White says that before working their fields, Acoma farmers call on them to protect their plants.

Oyoyewi—The younger of the War Twins.

prayer stick—The primary mode of communicating with rain spirits (Katsinas), they are carved from specific living trees or hollow reeds, and decorated with cotton string, appropriate colors, and feathers, all indicating the directional spirits to which they are addressed. Deposited at time-honored places as proper ritual etiquette for inviting spirits to reciprocate with blessings for the people, they embody prayer messages, can be gifts, and serve as invitations for Katsinas to visit.

Sage Basin—Known as *Washpashuka*, the second village site for Acoma migrants searching for Ha'ako.

Shipapu (also Shipap, or Sipapu)—The opening to the mythic, origin-related underworlds of Pueblo Indian cosmology. Some locate it in the Four Corners area, perhaps southeastern Colorado. It is also represented by a little cavity in some Pueblo kivas, often covered with a board on which dancers or ritualists stamp to send messages to the spirits underneath. Leslie A. White claims that "strictly speaking, Shipapu is the place in the fourth world below, inside the earth, where the people were at 'the beginning.'"

Spider Woman—An avatar of *Tsichtinako*, she is prominent in the myth's central section, where she assists the War Twins in their journey to see their father.

Tiamunyi—The son of primordial sister Nautsiti who marries her sister, Iatiku. The first man born to the leading Antelope clan and called "father of Katsina."

Tsichtinako—At other Keresan-speaking Pueblos, this central female deity is referred to variously as "Thought Woman," "Creator of All," and "Spider Woman," and by scholar Jay Miller as "Deified Mind."

Tsitsanits—Known as "Chief" of the first Katsinas.

Tule Lake—Known as *Ashthinahawgisha*, the third village settled by Acoma migrants in their search for Ha'ako, their ultimate resting place.

Uchtsiti—The male deity sometimes described as the "father" of the primordial sisters.

War Chief—Also known as "Country Chief," who rules "outside" the pueblo. Serving a one-year term, he is joined by two more "outside" officers. They are attended to by two cooks, who according to White are "usually men of considerable force of character and are always vigorous conservatives." They preserve old traditions, visit springs, leave offerings at critical locations in the Acoma cultural landscape, alert the kiva groups when to prepare for performances, and protect medicine men.

War Twins—Also known as the Warrior Twins or Hero Twins. Most Pueblo myths feature the pair, known at Acoma as Masewi (the elder) and Oyoyewi (the younger). They were sired by the Sun, who impregnated their mother with a ray of light. Their journey to find their father and acquire magical weapons is a classic epic among a number of southwestern tribes. These culture heroes guide migrants, slay monsters, and maintain rainfall. Ambivalent characters, they cleared the landscape of monsters for the first Acoma people, but their innate ferocity can go too far. Once the fight with the Katsinas is over and relations between cosmic realms are resolved, their tasks are done. Unable to live as common folk, they disappear into rocks on the east side of Acoma's mesa.

Wenimats—The location west of Acoma, in Zuni country, where most of the Acoma Katsinas are said to live under a lake (the others have their appointed residences around Acoma mesa).

White House—Known as *Kacikatcutia*, this is the first of the villages established by Acoma migrants after leaving the mythic place of emergence.

Bibliography

Armstrong, Karen. *A Short History of Myth*. Edinburgh, Scotland: Canongate, 2005.

Bauman, Richard. *Verbal Art as Performance*. Prospect Heights, IL: Waveland Press, Inc., 1977.

Benedict, Ruth. "An Introduction to Zuni Mythology." In Margaret Mead, *An Anthropologist at Work: Ruth Benedict*. Boston: Houghton Mifflin, 1959.

Densmore, Frances. *Music of Acoma, Isleta, Cochiti, and Zuni Pueblos*. Smithsonian Institution, Bureau of American Ethnology, Bulletin 165. Washington, DC: U.S. Government Printing Office, 1957.

Dozier, Edward P. *The Pueblo Indians of North America*. New York: Holt, Rinehart and Winston, 1970.

Dundes, Alan, ed. *Sacred Narrative: Readings in the Theory of Myth*. Berkeley: University of California Press, 1984.

Edelman, Sandra Prewitt. "Ascension Motifs and Reversals in Tewa Narratives." *Journal of Anthropological Research* 30, no. 1 (Spring 1974): 35–40.

Garcia-Mason, Velma. "Acoma Pueblo." In *Southwest*, vol. 9, edited by Alfonso Ortiz. *Handbook of North American Indians*. Washington, DC: Smithsonian Institution, 1979: 450–66.

Gutiérrez, Ramón A. *When Jesus Came, the Corn Mothers Went Away: Marriage, Sexuality, and Power in New Mexico, 1500–1846*. Stanford, CA: Stanford University Press, 1991.

Hatt, Gudmund. "The Corn Mother in America and in Indonesia." *Anthropos* 46 (1951): 853–914.

Jahner, Elaine. "Finding the Way Home: The Interpretation of American Indian Folklore." In *Critical Essays on Native American Literature*, edited by Andrew Wiget. Boston: G. K. Hall & Co., 1985.

Kroeber, Karl, ed. *Native American Storytelling: A Reader of Myths and Legends*. Malden, MA: Blackwell Publishing, 2004.

Lévi-Strauss, Claude, and Didier Eribone. *Conversations with Claude Lévi-Strauss*. Translated by Paula Wissing. Chicago: University of Chicago Press, 1991.

Malinowski, Bronislaw. "Myth in Primitive Psychology." In *Magic, Science, and Religion and Other Essays*. Garden City, NY: Doubleday Anchor Books, 1954.

Miller, Jay. "Deified Mind among the Keresan Pueblos." In *General and Amerindian Ethnolinguistics*, edited by Mary Ritchie Key and Henry M. Hoenigswald. Berlin: De Gruyter Mouton, 1989: 151–56.

Minge, Ward Alan. *Acoma: Pueblo in the Sky*. Rev. ed. Albuquerque: University of New Mexico Press, 2002.

Nabokov, Peter. *Architecture of Acoma Pueblo: The 1934 Historic American Buildings Survey Project*. Santa Fe, NM: Ancient City Press, 1986.

Ortiz, Alfonso. "A Uniquely American Legacy." In *The Princeton University Library Chronicle* 30, no. 3. Princeton, NJ: Princeton University Library, 1969.

Ortiz, Alfonso, and Richard Erdoes, eds. *American Indian Myths and Legends*. New York: Pantheon Books, 1984.

Ortiz, Simon. "Song, Poetry, and Language: Expression and Perception." Occasional Papers vol. 3, no. 5. Tsaile, AZ: Navajo Community College Press, 1977.

Radin, Paul. *Literary Aspects of North American Mythology*. Canada Geological Survey, Museum Bulletin 16, Anthropological Series 6 (1915).

Rooth, Anna Birgitta. "The Creation Myths of the North American Indians." *Anthropos* 52 (1957): 497–508.

Sebag, Lucien. *L'Invention du Monde Chez les Indiens Pueblos*. Paris: François Maspero, 1971.

Vecsey, Christopher. "The Emergence of the Hopi People." *American Indian Quarterly* 7 (Summer 1983): 69–92.

White, Leslie A. *The Acoma Indians*. Smithsonian Institution, Bureau of American Ethnology, 47th Annual Report, pp. 1–192. Washington, DC: U.S. Government Printing Office, 1932.

———. *New Material from Acoma*. Smithsonian Institution, Bureau of American Ethnology, Bulletin 136. Anthropological Papers, No. 32. Washington, DC: U.S. Government Printing Office, 1943.

———. "Summary of Field Work at Acoma." *American Anthropologist*. N.s. 30 (1928).

Wittfogel, Karl A., and Esther S. Goldfrank. "Some Aspects of Pueblo Mythology and Society." *The Journal of American Folklore* 56, no. 219 (1943): 17–30.

THE STORY OF PENGUIN CLASSICS

Before 1946 . . . "Classics" are mainly the domain of academics and students; readable editions for everyone else are almost unheard of. This all changes when a little-known classicist, E. V. Rieu, presents Penguin founder Allen Lane with the translation of Homer's *Odyssey* that he has been working on in his spare time.

1946 Penguin Classics debuts with *The Odyssey*, which promptly sells three million copies. Suddenly, classics are no longer for the privileged few.

1950s Rieu, now series editor, turns to professional writers for the best modern, readable translations, including Dorothy L. Sayers's *Inferno* and Robert Graves's unexpurgated *Twelve Caesars*.

1960s The Classics are given the distinctive black covers that have remained a constant throughout the life of the series. Rieu retires in 1964, hailing the Penguin Classics list as "the greatest educative force of the twentieth century."

1970s A new generation of translators swells the Penguin Classics ranks, introducing readers of English to classics of world literature from more than twenty languages. The list grows to encompass more history, philosophy, science, religion, and politics.

1980s The Penguin American Library launches with titles such as *Uncle Tom's Cabin* and joins forces with Penguin Classics to provide the most comprehensive library of world literature available from any paperback publisher.

1990s The launch of Penguin Audiobooks brings the classics to a listening audience for the first time, and in 1999 the worldwide launch of the Penguin Classics Web site extends their reach to the global online community.

The 21st Century Penguin Classics are completely redesigned for the first time in nearly twenty years. This world-famous series now consists of more than 1,300 titles, making the widest range of the best books ever written available to millions—and constantly redefining what makes a "classic."

The Odyssey continues . . .

The best books ever written

PENGUIN CLASSICS

SINCE 1946

Printed in the United States
by Baker & Taylor Publisher Services